Don't Ever Tell

Advance Praise for *Don't Ever Tell*

In *Don't Ever Tell*, author Christy Neal takes the reader along on her faith-filled journey from heartbreak to hope. Told with honesty and candor, this book will be a lifeline for women who are struggling to forgive themselves for infidelity and will thoughtfully guide them from regret to redemption.

> **—Mary O'Donohue**, Former post producer of "The Oprah Winfrey Show" and best-selling author of *When You Say "Thank You," Mean It*

I could not put this book down, and literally read it in one sitting . . . If you have cheated on a spouse or have ever been cheated on by a spouse, this book offers openness to bring understanding to the depth of the situation and is a must-read.

> **—Michelle Moore**, Award-winning author, speaker, and podcast host of "God Stories"

Don't Ever Tell is a great comeback story that encourages every woman to let go of shame and rebound from failure. Author Christy Neal shows us with her story that we can replace failure with a live-from-here mentality and fulfill the purpose God has for each of us.

> **—Monica Schmelter**, Host of *Christian Television Network's* daily show, "Bridges" and author of *Messy To Meaningful: Lessons From The Junk Drawer*

Christy has opened up her life to be an amazing help to others! God redeems and loves His children beyond our ability to understand, and I see this in Christy's life and testimony! This book is a must for everyone!

—**Tammy Daughtry**, Founder and CEO of
CoParenting International

Christy writes in such an inviting way. As she tells her story, she reminds us that others are crafting their stories daily as well. We are all different characters in different chapters of the life narratives of our brothers and sisters. Once I finished her book, I immediately assessed a few relationships in my life and changed the way I interact with some people very close to me. I realized that I had potentially withheld some of God's greatest treasure from those that I love—His grace. I am thankful that Christy is bold with her pen and open with her experience.

—**Taft Ayers**, Director of Business
Development at WAYFM

Christy Neal, a dynamic and extraordinarily real Christian woman, delivers a powerful message of healing, self-forgiveness, and internal restructure after the potential devastating effects of an affair. Her transparent message delivers to readers what few authors have been willing to do; share the ugly truth in a way the sheds light and hope into the life of those wanting to find their way out of a dark season in their life. I highly recommend her book.

—**Amy R. Butler**, Author of
U-Turn in the Single Lane

Whether you have been down the road of adultery or not, you will be inspired by the humility and courage found in Christy Neal's book, *Don't Ever Tell*. I applaud her for looking beyond the shame and stepping out to share her story so openly and honestly. We all struggle in some form or fashion and this book is a reminder that we can overcome darkness by the power of God's grace. Christy is truly a voice of hope!

—**Connie Smith**, Author and creator of the
Never Lose Heart book series

In her book, *Don't Ever Tell*, gifted author and speaker, Christy Neal, connects with those who have shared a similar experience. Through the art of storytelling, Christy gives hope to Christians who have fallen into what they believe is an unforgivable sin. Christy shares transparently and genuinely from her heart to help others overcome guilt and shame.

—**Amber Davis**, Author of *FLIGHT* and podcast
host of "bENCOURAGEd Today"

Don't Ever Tell is a book that every married woman should read. Christy does a phenomenal job of showing you how the path to adultery can start off innocently. I literally could not put the book down. I read it front to cover in one sitting. I feel this book can offer a lot of healing for those who have already been through adultery, whether they were the one that had the affair or they were cheated on. Christy spared no detail on her journey but did not sensationalize the act of adultery. In fact, anyone who reads this book will realize that we all fall short and need grace and redemption in our life.

—**Amanda Roberts**, Christian women's leader and founder of "The Ball In The Fall" Women's Conference

Christy Neal's riveting account of her own transgressions illustrates the danger signs that many ignore. Her genuine transparency reveals the true heart of a changed woman.

—**Leeann Cooper**, President of Ring of Faith Ministries and co-host of *Christian Television Network's* show, "Ring of Faith"

It takes courage to face our actions; it requires great courage to share how our actions led to redemption. My first husband committed adultery and wouldn't repent. As I've journeyed with Christy in *Don't Ever Tell*, I've witnessed "the other side," and it is not pain free. What unifies everyone's story is the need for the redeeming love of God. Thank you Christy, for loudly proclaiming who God is through the sharing of your story.

—**Lisa Miller-Rich**, Pastor and author of *218 Ways to Own Joy*

This book is a true offering. It is both gut wrenching and uplifting at the same time. It is never preachy, only told with true integrity. Christy has written a beautiful memoir and love letter to Jesus Christ. I whole-heartedly recommend this book to anyone and everyone who may need a reminder that God really does work in mysterious ways.

—**Sarah Vickery**, Nashville, TN

Don't Ever Tell was almost like reading my own story. I couldn't put it down. The raw truth in this book of how easily an affair can happen when someone is vulnerable and the temptation presents itself is spot on! Christy writes about how she prays for a woman to be placed into her life to minister to her that's been through the same thing, and I believe God chose Christy a long time ago for just this ministry to help women like her. This book could also be used to help women who might see an affair in the making and put a stop to it before it goes too far. Her book has been a blessing to me, and I know so many others will feel the same way.

—**Teresa Jablonski**, Mt. Juliet, TN

don't ever TELL

A Message of Hope, Healing, and Redemption After Adultery

CHRISTY NEAL

NEW YORK

LONDON • NASHVILLE • MELBOURNE • VANCOUVER

Don't Ever Tell

A Message of Hope, Healing, and Redemption After Adultery

Published in New York, New York, by Morgan James Publishing. Morgan James is a trademark of Morgan James, LLC. www.MorganJamesPublishing.com

Scripture quotations are taken from the Holy Bible, New International Version®, NIV®. Copyright © 1973, 1978, 1984, 2011 by Biblica, Inc.® Used by permission of Zondervan. All rights reserved worldwide. www.zondervan.com. The "NIV" and "New International Version" are trademarks registered in the United States Patent and Trademark Office by Biblica, Inc.®

Scripture quotations marked (NLT) are taken from the Holy Bible, New Living Translation, copyright © 1996, 2004, 2007 by Tyndale House Foundation. Used by permission of Tyndale House Publishers, Inc., Carol Stream, Illinois 60188. All rights reserved.

The use of additional translations is noted within the manuscript.
ISBN 9781631951589 paperback
ISBN 9781631951596 eBook
Library of Congress Control Number: 2020936959

Cover Design by:
Megan Dillon
megan@creativeninjadesigns.com

Interior Design by:
Chris Treccani
www.3dogcreative.net

Morgan James is a proud partner of Habitat for Humanity Peninsula and Greater Williamsburg. Partners in building since 2006.

Get involved today! Visit
MorganJamesPublishing.com/giving-back

For my sweet Girlie,
may you never doubt your inner self;
may you always have love in your heart
and a smile on your face;
may you always be surrounded with family
and genuine friends
who encourage you, laugh with you,
and dream with you;
may you always have confidence in your choices;
may you never let someone else dictate
how you feel about yourself;
may you never take advice from someone
whose shoes you would not be willing to fill. . .
and may you have total freedom to
live your life without the bondage of
guilt, shame, distrust, and fear.
This book is for you, My Love.
You are a born leader.
I believe in you, and I know you
will be a world changer!

Contents

Acknowledgments

First and foremost, thank you to my Lord and Savior, Jesus Christ, for redeeming me through His blood. Thank You for giving me this mission. I am honored and scared to death all at the same time. You instructed me to write this book. I did as You asked. I know it will reach whoever You need it to reach. I love You. You are my Best Friend, my Spiritual Husband, my Father, my Brother, my Counselor, and my Keeper. "Thank You" will never be enough. Please help me be a better servant to You every day that You bless me with here on this earth.

Second, to my family, I love you with all of my heart. You didn't choose to be attached to my mess, but you were. Thank you for handling it about as well as any family could. Thank you to my amazing Mom (Peggy Lindsley-Lambert) and Dad (Bob Pittman) who I am so blessed to belong to. I know you two aren't perfect, but you are perfect for me. Thank you for loving me no matter what, even though I know I let you down. I will do my best to never let that happen again. I cherish you both more than you know. Thank you to my Step Mom (Debbie Pittman) for loving me as your own. Thank you for teaching me how to be a good bonus mom. I would be clueless without you. To my dear Sister (Traci Pittman Williams), I know your world was flipped upside down when I was born, but I am so glad we have each other. In my mind, you are the epitome of what a sister should be. There for me always, judging me never, and a best friend in my corner. Thank you. To my Bubba (Les Williams), I always wanted a brother growing up and Traci chose well. Thank you for all the talks and discussions when I didn't know who to turn to for an outside man's opinion.

Third, thank you to my loyal friends who stood by me when most everyone else was walking away. You loved me through the poor choices and the pain of getting back up. When I told you about my mission to write this book, many of you kept me accountable by asking, "How is the book coming?" It took me forever and a day to finish the race, but it is finally complete! I could not have done it without your encouragement. Thank you for believing in me and for loving me, even when that was difficult to do. Your unconditional love was a key part to my healing. I love you all: Jenny Loftis, Carrie Davis, Kevin Burke, Janell Bunt, Jennifer Clanton Holaday, Jennifer Woody Loza, Richard McClellan, Josh McCory, Will Cook, Dew Wyatt, Tammy Onedera, Lori Bumpas, Jessica Benthall Schwieger, Linda Benthall Zelnik, and Amanda Bowers.

A special thank you to Alice Sullivan and Cortney Donelson, my editors, who are complete rock stars! Thank you to Morgan James Publishing for bringing my book to the shelves in hopes others will glean wisdom and hope from my story.

And finally, thank you to all the women who have allowed me to mentor you. You know who you are. It has been a true honor getting to know you. Your strength in sharing your story and courage in seeking help motivated me to complete this daunting project. Each of you contributed a piece of your heart to this story. It represents us all. Each of you helped me realize just how needed this message was. We now have a voice. Scarlet and scorned but never silent.

Foreword

"**D**on't let those words ever pass your lips again. You are glorifying Satan." The stern look on her face matched her tone of voice. Sister Gale traveled the world as a women's minister leader, so she must be right. I was only nineteen. I knew I'd get into more trouble if I told anyone else about getting raped at five.

Decades later, after the isolation and abuse had made me suicidal, I finally got help and started to tell my story to my counselor and support system. As I shed the shame and guilt, I found healing and broke the cycles of abuse that had been destroying my life.

Reading Scarlett's story was a reminder of how adultery and pain had been a large part of my life. My husband had an affair off-and-on for five years with my best friend before the dissolve of our fifteen-year marriage. After my divorce, I was date raped and became pregnant. And later, I had an emotional affair with a married man that ended when the kissing started. I only ended it then because I knew the excruciating pain of being "the wife" and refused to become "the other woman."

As I read *Don't Ever Tell* and faced the pain of my past, I felt more healing happening. Hot tears poured down my cheeks. I wanted to get every ounce of healing God had for me in this raw, vulnerable story of brokenness and redemption.

Adultery may be the subject directly tackled in this book, but it represents any type of sin we get tempted into. We're all susceptible in the right (or wrong) circumstances. Anyone who believes they are better than one particular sin is dangerously close to a destructive fall off of their own pedestal of self-righteousness and pride.

My silence almost killed me. My pride set me up for a fall. But God! How I wish I'd been able to read *Don't Ever Tell* much earlier in my journey. Because this "cautionary memoir" is also a *healing journey*.

> "And they overcame him [Satan] by the blood of the Lamb and by the word of their testimony, and they did not love their lives to the death." (Revelation 12:11, KJV)

Beautifully written, *Don't Ever Tell* will challenge you, inspire you, unmask you, and give you hope for new healing and redemption. I'm incredibly proud of Christy for sharing her raw testimony of God's love and redemption. She unmasks the enemy's tactics. She shines light on the enemy's lies and shares God's truth instead, so we can find healing.

This is absolutely the best book I've ever read on this subject! Christy, your transparency is so refreshing. Thanks for contributing to my ongoing healing. You're a huge blessing.

Paula Mosher Wallace
President of Bloom In The Dark, Inc., 501c3
Ordained Minister, Producer, Television Host, Author

Introduction:

Simply Stated

I was called to write this book. I was called to tell my story—bare my ugly for all to see. Because my story isn't about me anymore. My story is for all those hopeless women who feel they have messed up and are beyond repair. The ones who don't know how to forgive themselves or don't know if they ever can.

One day while leaving the gym, a phrase on the locker room door caught my eye. It said the following: "No life is worthless that lightens the burden of another." That simple statement wraps up my intent for this book. I want to lighten the burden of those who have walked in my shoes, those who have been tempted to walk in my shoes, and those who have walked in these shoes and hidden them away in the darkest closet they could find, still fearful that one day someone will find them and know their secret.

I am willing to be the voice I so desperately needed to hear all those years ago.

My name is Scarlett, and this is my story.

Chapter 1

Peek-a-Boo:
Hiding from the Truth

"There is no pillow so soft as a clear conscience."
—French proverb

Josie Rose is two and a half years old.

As my lover quietly rolled out of the back of my SUV, I entertained my sweet baby girl with a game of peek-a-boo. I strategically placed the fuzzy blanket over her head so she wouldn't notice the man who wasn't her daddy exiting our vehicle. "Peek-a-Boo!" I would say loudly as he closed the hatchback door to muffle the sound of the latch. I removed the blanket playfully. She giggled. I sighed with relief. Another visit was successfully hidden from my toddler and from the neighbors.

Tate would sometimes come to my house and visit during Josie's naptime. While she was slumbering, we were escaping reality and frolicking in our personal fantasy land. Everything was peaceful there. No responsibilities or expectations. No bills or jobs or parenting or discussions of needs going unmet. Just two lost souls accepting the other fully. It had become our bliss.

Just moments earlier, Tate was hiding in the back of my SUV for the short ride up the street to his truck. Now I could see him in my side-view mirror as he crouched down beside my vehicle, waved, and snuck off to his truck. My heart sank to see him leave. Not for what I had done, but because I wasn't sure when I would see him again. He had become my lifeline. My source of survival in a marriage that was as lifeless as my rose garden in the backyard. Just like the roses, my marriage had been left to die a slow, painful death from neglect. Being starved of attention and affection, I felt as lifeless as those once-beautiful petals.

But when Tate was there, I felt renewed, fresh, vibrant, sexy, desired, adventurous, appreciated, and loved. I felt alive! And in a way, I had never felt alive before. I felt like I had been starved of food for months, and finally, someone noticed me and cared enough to throw me a bag of cookies. But not just any cookies—the best darn cookies I had ever tasted!

These cookies were my new truth. In fact, these newly discovered cookies made me feel lied to. In all my years of Sunday school, youth group, church, devotionals, and Christian college, no one ever told me this type of cookie even existed—the sweetness of a passionate romance, the feeling of my thoughts, my desires, and my heart truly being known. I thought this kind of relationship was only found in the movies. Where had it been all my life?

It didn't matter now. All I knew was that this was exactly what I needed to survive my stay-at-home haze.

Of course, I would only do this for a season. *Just a season.* I needed something to break up the monotony. *Just a season*, I would tell myself.

Deep in my heart, I wanted Christian Robert, my love, my husband. But he had disappeared. The man I'd fallen in love with had left—vanished. And there wasn't a trace of him anywhere to be found.

After the birth of our daughter, Josie Rose, instead of becoming a playful new father, Christian seemed to turn more serious and fatherly toward me with every passing month. Further still from the goofy, fun-loving, all-American boy I fell for in college. When our daughter was only several months old, I realized I didn't even recognize the man I had fallen in love with all those years ago. He had lost his smile and his energy. He didn't laugh anymore, and he made it a point to not look at me when I was being silly. He acted as if he were a seventy-year-old elder of a conservative church and not a thirty-something-year-old husband and new father. In fact, I felt we hardly talked anymore unless it was about Josie or other people and their goings-on.

I didn't understand why. What could have created such a change in his personality? Was he not thrilled with being a new father to our beautiful daughter? Did he no longer find me attractive now that I was the mother of his child?

Was I no longer enthralling because I wasn't working outside of the home? The personal rejection, along with the silence, became too much to bear.

With no answers from him and none to be found on my own, I cried a lot. I missed my Christian Robert. I missed how he enjoyed me. I missed his laugh and his silly grandpa jokes. I missed him being interested in me.

He was great with Josie, and he did help around the house, but as she got older he seemed to slip further into depression. I felt like a single mother when his work was particularly busy. Other times I felt completely alone even when he was home. I don't think Christian realized how absent he was.

I was dying a slow emotional death, starved of attention that my inner child so desperately needed. It was all too familiar of a feeling, and those deep-seated insecurities crept back to the surface.

As a child, I hadn't received much attention from my father. I remembered how alone and confused I felt. Now, more than twenty years later, I felt those same fears again. It was as if I were drowning in silence and no one saw me or could hear my cries for help. And in the months of being ignored, all of those disappointments and fears created the perfect internal storm—I fell prey to the one sin I swore I would *never* commit. The sin of my own father, and the sin of my mother's father. I committed adultery. I betrayed my husband, my family, and worst of all . . . myself.

Looking myself in the eyes in a mirror became harder and harder. I was beginning to no longer recognize myself.

The woman I was proud of. The woman I had worked so hard to become.

The devil had lied to me. And I believed every deceitful whisper.

Christian may never cheat on me with another woman, I thought to myself, *but he cheats on me daily with his computer, with TV, with fantasy football, with sports, with poker, and with finances.* I nearly felt justified in my actions. I felt so alone. My husband was a robot, and a shell of the person I married. He was under the same roof with us, but he walked around without showing any emotion. He didn't see me, and he was missing out on our beautiful baby girl.

I couldn't reach him. I didn't understand what had happened to us. I started to seek help yet again. Despite earlier failed attempts, I had to continue my quest to find a counselor who could save our marriage.

Chapter 2

2x4

*"You will always pass failure
on your way to success."*
—**Mickey Rooney**

Josie Rose is just shy of two years old.

I sat on the counselor's couch like a scared rabbit. I had to sign several papers before we began. It felt more like I was at a legal office. She seemed so business-like, drilling me with questions from across the room about who I was and why I was there. There were no warm fuzzies with this counselor, unlike the two before her. No small talk. It all seemed so impersonal.

When she finally finished filling out her paperwork on her new prospective client, she took a seat in front of me. Then she looked me straight in the eyes and asked, "So, why are you here?" It was very direct. She wasn't looking for my childhood history, my family dynamics, or any Southern sugar-coated answer. She wanted to know exactly why I was there. It was a "Let's cut to the chase"

6

kind of question. Before I answered, I remember thinking, "This is the woman my mom suggested I go see? This is the Church of Christ Christian counselor who has helped so many hurting couples?"

At the moment the thought of her being able to help anyone was hard to fathom. I sat staring at a very cold, very direct woman who was on a mission for truth in forty-five minutes. So I decided to lay it on her. I had not tried that approach so far with the other counselors, but I vomited out my situation like soured milk. I told her all of it: Christian's neglect, his rejection, my abandonment issues from my father and stepfather, including all of the times I had directly told Christian Robert that men were giving me attention and that I was starting to like it and that I didn't want to cheat on him, that I didn't want to be like my dad. And how the next morning it would be like we hadn't talked about anything. I told her how I felt like I was going crazy. Then I told her about my friend, how I met him through church, how our marriages were both so alike. How we connected and understood each other because of our similar dysfunctional family dynamics. How I didn't want to stop seeing him but I knew I needed to. About how we were becoming close friends, and about how I just couldn't reach Christian, and how I had tried everything except blatantly hanging a sign across the house that said, "Hello! I am about to have an affair!"

She sat quietly, intently looking at me as if she could see through me. She jotted down a few notes. When I was finished dumping my internal baggage, she barely paused.

As if she had heard the story many times before, she said, "Well, it appears you need to hit your husband upside the head with a two-by-four. He will either listen and change, or he won't. If he doesn't, then you chalk it up to a failed marriage and move on."

I thought I was going to fall off of her quack couch! Chalk it up to a failed marriage?! I thought, "This woman is Church of Christ?" Who was she to talk so nonchalantly about my situation? Did she not hear me? I was about to start a full-blown affair. An affair with someone at church!

And then, as if she saw the utter terror and confusion on my face, she said this: "Do you understand what I mean by 'hit him with a two-by-four'? I see this a lot, Scarlett. And unfortunately, they either listen and change, or they do not. If you are as desperate as you say you are, you need to decide what your two-by-four looks like. Use it and see if it takes. If it doesn't, you have a decision to make. I have been doing this for over twenty years. Sometimes marriages fail. I wish I could say they are all saved, but it just isn't reality."

Needless to say, I could not get off her couch fast enough. I felt like I handed that woman $100, told her my life story, and then she hit me with a Mack truck!

I was in complete shock. A failed marriage? That was not in the plan. That was not an option! I thought she would have the answers. I thought she would tell me this was normal and just do *X, Y,* and *Z,* and I would get back on track. I am not sure what I expected from her . . . but it wasn't what I got!

I crawled back into my car, shaking like an abused puppy, and sat there unable to move, trying to grasp reality. Had that really just happened? Did I hear what I thought I heard? I was dumbfounded.

A two-by-four? What did that look like? She mentioned leaving him for a period of time to get his attention, and then he would either listen or he wouldn't.

Sitting in the driver's seat, gripping my steering wheel, I realized I had, in fact, gotten my money's worth. I was suddenly tired of opinions. I just wanted God Himself to come counsel me, comfort me, keep me, and tell me exactly what to do. But He didn't.

After all, we have free will. *We* have to choose.

As bewildered as I was at that moment, she was right about one thing. I needed to choose my two-by-four.

Chapter 3

Deeper Still

"The challenge in life isn't staying out of the rough,
it's getting out once you're in it."

—Chinese fortune

Josie is two years and a couple months old.

While I left the counselor's office with a small feeling of resolve, it soon crumbled, and I felt defeated once more. The cold-blooded therapist hadn't helped my current situation. The session frightened me and caused me to shut down instead of face reality. I internally processed what I had heard from the counselor and what I was feeling when I went home, but I did not tell Christian about this counselor . . . not about what she really said. That would have meant me telling him about Tate.

Yes, I had been telling Christian for some time that I was sad, lonely, and scared. He knew I was unhappy and thought it was a symptom of being a new mom. He dismissed it. After that counseling session, I decided to ignore the problem just like Christian had. He acted like everything was fine, so I decided to do the same. It was an easy way to avoid working on our marriage.

I didn't talk to any other counselors for nearly six months. I was afraid of their advice. I just wanted to carry on and forget that my marriage was slowly falling apart. I wanted to forget my unhappiness. So I did exactly that. I carried on like life at home was good, perfect, in fact.

I played the part of a happy housewife. I kept a perfectly clean house, cooked dinners each night, and made sure our home was comfortable, clean, and relaxing by the time Josie's daddy came home. But during the day, my extra time was spent e-mailing, messaging, and talking with my friend. And if I wasn't communicating with him, I was daydreaming about him.

It was easy to fantasize about this "perfect" man. He was fun, exciting, energetic, charming, fit, talkative, inquisitive, successful, daring, and smart. I felt he was interested in me; I felt heard; I felt seen for the first time in a long time. I also felt wanted and desired. And it was thrilling and diverting. It was a dangerous place to be. Separating my daydreams from my reality was getting harder and harder. I was consumed.

Some nights I cried myself to sleep because Christian would actually *want* to touch me, and I couldn't bear the thought of it. If he initiated anything, I would turn over, away from him, and cry silently. He would fall asleep quickly and never notice me crying. I learned from my father not to cry, especially in front of others. I felt so distant from Christian, as if I was sleeping next to a stranger.

One night I decided to talk to him about how I was feeling. I was sitting on his lap in his recliner in our bonus room, and I tried to make myself be intimate with him. I started kissing on his neck. He started kissing me back, but I just couldn't do it. I just couldn't give myself to him. I pulled back and told Christian—my own husband—that I just couldn't make love to him anymore. I told him I felt so distant and that it was like trying to get intimate with a stranger. I told him again that men were giving me attention and that I was actually starting to like it. I told him I was scared and that I needed him to go to counseling *with* me because something was *wrong* with our relationship. I told him that I didn't want to cheat on him as my father had on my mother. He looked at me with compassion and told me that it would be all right. He held me and told me he loved me.

But again, the next morning, when I looked sad in the kitchen fixing breakfast he asked what was wrong. It was as if we hadn't talked at all. It was as if he didn't remember last night. It was as if since it had been discussed, it was over. But it wasn't over!

I felt crazier than ever. He went to work and I took care of my sweet girl. I felt as if Josie and I were alone in this big world and no one would understand my situation. From the outside looking in, we looked like the perfect family. But secretly, silently, we were far from it. My precious daughter was my reason for staying. I wanted so much more for her than what I had as a child. The only confidante I had was my new friend.

Tate would listen. Tate would console me. Tate would understand. And during Josie's naptime, he started coming to visit.

Chapter 4

A Burger with a Side
of Ultimatum

*"Indifference and neglect often do much more
damage than outright dislike."*

—**J. K. Rowling**, *Harry Potter and the Order of the Phoenix*

Josie Rose is almost two and a half years old.

Several months after the emotional part of the affair began, I mustered up the courage to start seeing yet another counselor. This one was free, and I figured it was worth a shot since I wouldn't be out any money. By this point, I was attempting to seek help in any way I could. Some days I just needed to unload on someone completely outside of my circle.

On this particular day in early fall, I missed my appointment on purpose. I was so tired of being on the couch alone. This problem was not just mine—it was ours. But I couldn't seem to get that through Christian's thick head. Maybe he felt that since I was from a broken, dysfunctional family, I was the one who needed help. He was wrong. We were both broken and lacking in our own way.

It felt good to miss counseling. It was a passive-aggressive way to show how angry I was at Christian for putting all of this work on our marriage on my shoulders. And just to make sure he knew, I decided that night at dinner I would tell him I missed my appointment, and I would give him an ultimatum. He would either listen, or he wouldn't—just like that last crazy counselor had advised.

Christian wanted to go to a new burger place downtown. We had never been there before, and I didn't care where we went. I had no appetite, especially since I was a mixture of nerves and frustration, but he was craving a good ground round. We sat through most of our dinner just sharing small talk about day-to-day life. It was the usual "How was your day?" routine. As I expected, nothing exciting was ever going on with him at work. After all, how exciting can accounting be? And nothing too exciting was going on for me as a stay-at-home mom either. Well, nothing I could tell him about, anyway. The boredom of the conversation nearly lulled me into a state of slumber. But instead I blurted out, "I missed counseling today."

"You did?" Christian replied, sounding curious. "Why did you do that?" he inquired while finishing a bite of his hamburger.

I stalled a moment, wanting him to squirm. But he didn't, he just kept on eating. "I made a decision today," I proclaimed, waiting for a response.

"And what is that?" he asked in between bites.

"I decided I am not going to counseling anymore," I stated matter-of-factly. I sat and waited for his reaction. It seemed I was always trying to get any show of emotion out of my husband, like I could somehow provoke a response that indicated he cared. In the next few seconds of silence, I thought he might be mad or upset that I didn't go. But that wasn't the case.

Christian looked up from his plate with no sense of urgency whatsoever. "Is that so?" he said casually. "And why did you decide that? Are you feeling okay?"

Internally I was coming unglued. *Feeling okay?! Feeling okay? No, I'm not feeling okay!* I wanted to scream. But since we were in a public place, I firmly said, "I'm sick of going by myself, Christian. Can't you see this is *our* problem, not *my* problem? I'm not going back until you go with me!"

He spoke up and said, "Okay, okay. I hear you."

And that was that.

I thought from that conversation that Christian would finally get what was going on. I really thought he would step up and call a counselor and set up an appointment for both of us. After all, he was the more responsible one, never paying a bill late or forgetting an appointment. But I was wrong.

After that night, after the burger and the side of ultimatum, he never mentioned counseling to me again. Not once. I took it as a sign that he didn't really want to go and he didn't care enough to fight for me. That dinner conversation was the straw that broke the camel's back. It awoke a monster in me that had been lying dormant for years.

Each day that passed from that night on, I grew more and more angry. All the neglect from my father, all of the abandonment from my stepfather, all of the rejection from Christian, all of the conversations that weren't heard, all of my cries for help that fell on deaf ears, all of the trying to be perfect to avoid my family's dysfunctional patterns, everything I had chosen, everything I had learned over the years about God and about putting others first . . . all of it was consumed by an evil nemesis—a desperate woman fueled by years of pent-up pain. All of the doubts and disappointment, the neglect and rejection, were digested into the belly of this beastly need within. Deep down into my core, I was sick of being unheard, sick of being good, sick of waiting, sick of asking, sick of working, sick of sacrificing, and sick of talking!

Starved for attention and redemption, my inner woman would have whatever she wanted. She wanted control. She was spiteful and wanted to be seen, heard, appreciated, desired, selfish, and all powerful. The abomination grew within. I was too tired to fight her.

So she took over. And her wrath was about to be unleashed.

Chapter 5

A Nap a Day
Keeps the Blues Away

*"Each one of us is born with a box of matches
inside us, but we can't strike them all by ourselves."*
—**Laura Esquivel**, *Like Water for Chocolate*

My sweet girlie is almost three years old.

Naptime had become my lifeline. After Christian's inaction to my ultimatum, I just didn't care anymore. If he didn't care, I didn't care. And finally I gave in. I gave in to my feelings for Tate. I stopped fighting to do what was right. I gave in to my flesh as the devil convinced me that I deserved a little fun. *Just a season*, he would whisper to me again and again. *Just a season of fun. You deserve it. You work so hard.*

I began to agree with these thoughts and told myself it would only be for a season . . . *A season of fun*, I thought to myself. It wouldn't last long—just a few months. I just needed something for me. I just needed a small escape from reality.

Our naptime visits had evolved over the months from friendly conversation over coffee at the kitchen table to holding hands on the couch and pecks on the cheek and forehead. Our discussions intrigued me, and it was so nice to talk with someone who understood me and where I was coming from. With Christian, conversation was now so bland. I would try to get him to talk, but he was usually anxious to watch TV, get on his computer, or look at our finances. I felt many times he chose those things over me, like he was cheating on me with technology and sports.

Tate had become my drug of choice,
and I had no interest in rehab.

But Tate gave me his undivided attention. So much so that I would sometimes become uneasy with the way he looked at me so longingly, so directly in the eyes. I wasn't used to being seen . . . observed . . . studied. Tate studied everything about me. His eyes were wild with intense curiosity. He wanted to know it all, and I was flattered.

Soon there were longer hugs, and we sat closer together when he visited. I could feel the heat from Tate's body every time we were near each other. I felt drawn to him like there was a magnetic force between us. My skin felt like it might burst with excitement every time he touched me. Our visits spanned over a year before we both fully gave into our desires of the flesh—but once that happened, there was no turning back.

I began to live for naptime. When it wasn't naptime, I daydreamed about the next naptime. Now, don't get me wrong, I loved my time with my Girlie. We always had a great time. We played, we laughed, we ran errands, we chased each other at the park, went to the pool, had play dates with little friends, read silly children's books, snuggled, had tickle-ramas, and then we played some more! I would not trade those years with Josie for anything. And to this day, I am so thankful that Christian and I were able to keep our little Rose out of childcare.

However, Josie's naptime had evolved into my *playtime*. It was my time to do what felt good to me for a change. My time to do whatever I liked to do. Unfortunately, what I liked to do was with someone else's husband from my church.

As terrible as that sounds, Tate took care of me. He made me feel wanted. He made me feel chosen. He made me feel like "not-a-mom" for that hour or two each day that he visited. He was drawn to my free-spirited nature and sense of humor. I loved to have fun and he did too. This was passionate; it was carnal; it was adult love—wild and intimate. It was also rebellious. And it was exactly what I had been taught *all* my life was wrong . . . and I think in a sick, twisted way, I loved that.

I was finally experiencing life on my terms. I was choosing for myself. I was exploring. I was stepping out of the lines for the first time in my life. And it felt amazing!

Like a caged animal that was finally set free, I could roam, run, live, hunt, kill, and eat when I wanted.

I loved every second of my time with Tate. And even though I knew how wrong it was, I could *not* get enough. I was borderline addicted to our connection and how he made me feel—how he made my mind and my body feel. And for a "goodie-two-shoe, conservative, naïve, Christian young woman" it was my paradise. My secret world. Not the world I was raised in, not the dos-and-don'ts of the church—my personal blazing hot planet.

It was mine. *It was ours.* Our very own world where whatever we wanted of the other we could have. I grew attached very quickly to this season of fun. Tate became my drug of choice. And I had no interest in rehab.

Chapter 6

Service with a Smile

"I never dreamed I could go from a simple Mary Kay delivery to delusional. I guess it speaks to how lonely and lost I was."

—Scarlett Rose

Josie Rose is one year and five months old.

I had to make at least $500 a month to be able to stay at home with Josie. Neither Christian nor I wanted Josie in daycare, so we decided I would quit my full-time job to become a full-time mom. As hard as this new stay-at-home gig was, I was not about to put Josie in childcare if I didn't have to, but we still needed some extra income. So we decided that I would ramp up my Mary Kay efforts to bring in the needed funds. I started selling in our first year of marriage. Things were going well. Some months I even brought in close to $1,000! I was thrilled to help out, and the weekly sales meetings were a nice break from my normal mom duties.

Josie's second Christmas was near, and I decided to set a lofty goal for myself. I wanted to do an open house, and my goal was to make $2,000 in sales to help out with purchasing gifts. This was a large goal compared to my open houses in years past, but I was determined to make it happen. So I planned the day, prepared invitations, cleaned my house, and set up my retail store in the dining room.

I invited everyone I knew, and several ladies from church came by to support my event. I was so thankful to all the neighbors and friends who came by to shop, and I was proud that I earned close to my targeted amount. I only needed about $400 more to have the biggest open house total I had ever had!

I had no idea that the next day's delivery would change my life forever.

Christian and I brainstormed on ways to reach the hefty goal of two grand. At the time, we were fairly new members of a decent-sized church not far from our home. We were regular attendees, were involved in a young couple's Sunday school class, and had just started attending a home church group. Christian Robert had an idea for me to call the husbands in our class and home church group to make sure they had all of their Christmas gifts together for their lovely brides. After all, he reminded me, men always wait to the last minute to shop. *True*, I thought to myself, wondering if he had done the same for me this year. It was a clever idea, so I started dialing.

I sold several gift sets and made almost $300 more toward my bottom line. As a last-ditch effort, I decided to e-mail any husbands I had not been able to reach by phone. I searched through the directory and gathered a few more names of men to reach out to. A couple of the husbands I had never met. But I didn't think it mattered, and I was definitely not afraid to ask for the business. After all, I had a challenge ahead of me, and I was determined to reach it!

Shortly following my afternoon e-mail blast, I had a response from a man named Tate who worked at some development group. He wanted to hear what ideas I had in mind. He admitted that he had not finished shopping for his wife, and he was very interested in the help, especially if I was doing the shopping, wrapping, and delivering for him. Excited that I might have another sale, I put together a few fabulous gift ideas and e-mailed them to him. Within minutes, I received the following response: "Great ideas! I will take one of each. Just send over the total."

My jaw literally dropped. I could not believe it! This was awesome! I remember jumping out of my office chair and screaming, "Woo hoo!" With this sale, I had surpassed my goal. I was ecstatic. I e-mailed him back, trying to remain calm, and asked him if he would like to pick the items up off of my porch where I had a drop-and-grab basket, or if he would like "service with a smile." With my bubbly innocent personality, I really had no idea what

I was getting into. He replied, "Definitely service with a smile."

"What a charming guy," I thought to myself. I went on to ask where he worked and discovered his office was conveniently located just around the corner from my house. "How funny," I thought. I let him know I would get everything together and drop off the goodies the following afternoon. I had no idea that the next day's delivery would change my life forever.

Chapter 7

Mesmerized

"Your habits will determine your future."
—Jack Canfield

Sweet Josie Rose is one year and five months old on the day we meet Tate.

I piled my Mary Kay deliveries for the day into my SUV, loaded up Josie, and hit the road. I figured my first stop of the day would be to Tate since his office was just around the corner. We pulled in, and I unloaded Josie and the goods. I had no idea what Tate looked like or who he was really. I had met his wife at previous church events, but couldn't place him in my mind. As we approached the office door, a gentleman opened the door before we could even knock. "Hi. I'm here to deliver something to Tate Rogers," I said politely, not knowing who this man was.

"That would be me," the tall, dark, and handsome stranger stated.

"Oh. Well, hello there. I'm Scarlett and this is Josie Rose," I replied. He looked me directly in the eyes with a confident grin on his face and said, "I know." He then explained that he had seen us around the church. I was immediately captivated by his charming smile and his dark bronze eyes. They seemed to look through me in a very mysterious way. We talked and talked and talked. The conversation flowed like we had known each other for years. It was very strange, and I recall not really wanting to leave. It was nice to talk to another grown-up for a change, and the conversation was so easy, unlike at home. It caught me off guard, and I remember both of us smiling quite a bit. Josie had only been walking for about a month, and she was toddling around the office everywhere. I started to feel like I was intruding on the workday, so I thanked him for his business, got my payment, and headed out for the next delivery. As I was driving away from Tate's office, I remember saying out loud to Josie, "Huh. That was interesting, Girlie."

No one wakes up one morning and says to themselves, "I think I'll have an affair today."

A couple of days passed, and I didn't think much about my encounter with Tate. That is until I received an e-mail from him one afternoon. To my surprise, he wrote thanking me again for the "service with a smile," and he wanted to know if I could put together a few more items for his female co-workers. I was thrilled at the opportunity to make yet another sale, but I was also surprised at how excited I was to see his name in my inbox.

From this second transaction, we started chatting via e-mail. It became something I looked forward to each day, wondering if I would hear from him. We shared jokes, and he cracked me up so easily. It wasn't long before we were e-mailing on a daily basis, sharing stories, asking and answering questions about the other, and sharing music. It was amazing how much we had in common.

Over the course of several months, we became very close through our communications. We would giggle when we saw each other at church, knowing that no one else knew that we were friends. It was a fun secret, almost like being in school and having a crush on someone. I can't speak for Tate, but I felt very innocent in communicating with him and had no intention of taking things where they ended up. But then again, no one wakes up one morning and says to themselves, "I think I'll have an affair today." It's something that slowly grows over time, like a seed that is planted and watered. Before you know it you have a bloom, and it's mesmerizing and new.

People want to focus on the dirtiness of affairs. They tend to only think about sex and the physical adultery involved. They tend to label it ugly and perverted. Now, don't mistake me, affairs *are* wrong. They are terrible and tragic and destructive, and some affairs definitely can be all about the physical aspects. There are people who only engage in affairs for sex.

However, the majority of the time, at least with believers who find themselves in an affair, it is about much more than sex. Many times there was a friendship first, then an emotional affair turned into a physical affair. I own the fact that my affair was wrong and there was no justification for those selfish choices. I also want to share insight that when two believers are having an affair, the sex isn't necessarily the focus for the two who are involved. There is often much more. There is a bond. There is a strong friendship. There is trust. Most often, there is a foundation of friendship, a commonality you can both stand on, and a shared faith. There is a similar need—a strong connection. There is an emotional void being filled. There is support and understanding within the relationship.

In many cases, there is no intention for a physical affair, especially on the woman's side, because women are often more emotionally charged. But there is curiosity. There are small, seemingly insignificant steps in a direction that you don't realize you are heading especially because you both believe you would *never* have an affair. There is a birth of daily habits. Then, before you know it, there are feelings and emotions. Then there is a partnership. There is a world that only belongs to the two of you. There is a loyalty to that world and to your secret. There is a safe haven in that world—a new creation—and you feel powerful there because it's your own. No one can take it from you or judge you there.

There is so much more to an affair than sex. It becomes a living, breathing organism that you want to sustain and nurture and protect because you are the only two who understand it. And then, you feel a dedication and a responsibility to each other to guard it against the outside world.

It becomes your high. But it isn't as easy to throw out like a drug or a drink because another person is involved and that person is someone you care deeply about.

I tell you this *not* to justify an affair—there is no justification—but to help you see how an affair begins and see how easily one can find themselves in a situation that was not intended. It is surprising how easy it can be to find oneself in the middle of a situation you *never* dreamed you'd be in. Perhaps my story will help you guard yourself against being subjected to the temptation of an affair. I challenge you to never say never. "Never" opens the window of opportunity for temptation.

Looking back, I would define an affair as two people who fill a void so deep for the other that they go against what they believe and they risk everything for just one more visit. Tate was my fix, my greatest need. And I couldn't just throw him away.

Chapter 8

Sin Is Fun

"When you misbehave, you miss out."
—**Scarlett Rose**

I felt like I had discovered a bar of euphoria-inducing chocolate. It was the best-tasting treat I had ever had! Why had no one told me this high existed? I felt as if I had been lied to. All these years I was taught that sin was bad. Sin weighed you down. "Don't do that, don't do this, only do this and that." Growing up in a conservative church, the main focus seemed to be the list of dos and don't-dos. But there was never any explanation of *why* you didn't do those things.

So here I was, the epitome of a member of a conservative church. The perfect young lady who had played by all the rules—and I mean *all* of them. I had never been drunk, never done drugs, never smoked, never slept around, and had never done anything else on the list of "don't dos." In fact, even as early as high school, everyone knew where I stood on those topics, so much so that parents were thrilled when I was the girl their child would be hanging out with. They knew that if their child was with Scarlett, there would be no drinking or drugs or mishaps occurring. I simply wouldn't put up with it. I was *that girl*—the "goodie-two-shoes." And to be honest, I didn't mind it at all. I was on a mission to *never* end up where my parents were—divorced. My parents were wonderful parents, but they weren't together. Even as a young child, I just knew *together* would be better.

I figured that if I loved God, played by all the rules, did all the right things, and didn't do the wrong things, my future family and I would be protected. I chose to go to a Christian university. I wanted to learn, not party. My goal was to graduate before getting married—if I even decided to wed at all. And I did just that. Although Christian and I met while we were in college, I waited six months after graduation to marry Christian. Just to make sure I couldn't live without him, I moved back to Nashville while he finished college out of state. I missed him terribly, and we decided after six months that we would marry.

We were both virgins when we married, successful graduates of the True Love Waits program. He had also played by all the rules growing up. He never drank, never did drugs, and didn't sleep around. After all, I had a tall list of qualifications that my future husband would have to meet before I signed up for a lifetime of love. I had worked hard to be who I was, and to *not* be who I wasn't, if that makes sense. I wanted someone who had worked equally as hard. I didn't want some jerk who had lived recklessly, slept around, drank, and did Lord knows what else to Lord knows who, only to want to find a sweet virgin to settle down with. No sir, wasn't going to happen. Christian Robert fit the bill perfectly. He was the checklist match I had waited for. Not to mention he had a family that was actually still together.

I fell in love with Christian and with his family. He was the real deal, and I was thrilled that God had made him just for me. I truly felt that way. We had survived the world of temptation in our youth, we had found each other, we had made it to our wedding day without getting pregnant, without getting drunk, and without getting high. We had arrived. Let the blessings flow! God would join us in holy matrimony, and the rest would be history. We loved God, loved each other, and loved life. From that point on, we would be blessed. It all sounds so cliché, but we truly bought into that theory . . . and many young couples have been united in the same bubble-type of environment.

Sometimes, I wonder if Christian and I were exactly where Satan wanted us. In our minds, we had arrived. And because of this, we let our guards down. We were a wide-open target for the devil. We were complacent. We were arrogant. We were lofty, we were so proud, and we felt untouchable. What a joke!

No one told us the real work began *after* the ceremony. No one told us how to maintain this gift that we had acquired, the gift of marriage. No one explained that now we had marks on our backs as believers and that the devil would be after our family. We literally arrived, got the trophy of marriage, and set it on the shelf. We never even dusted it! We would stop every so often, look at it, and say, "Wow. Look at that. Look what we did! We are so great." And then we would go about our ways, each day getting a little further from the other without even realizing it.

Looking back, we were almost destined to struggle. I went to counseling alone before we got married. That should have been a sign. We had problems with conversation in our dating years. I assumed (like many naïve young brides) that it would get better once we were married. I felt that since I was such a good communicator (my degree was in communications) I would rub off on him. But it didn't happen.

Jobs came, apartments were chosen, friends were made, church was there and checked off, a house was bought, a baby came, different jobs were taken, roles changed, bills piled up, debt accrued, worry entered, conversations stopped, resentment built, loneliness knocked, eyes rolled, distance grew, more debt accrued, disappointment moved in, temptation whispered, TVs and PCs and cell phones were always on, and attention to detail was turned off. With all the distractions, sin moved in like a houseguest who promised he would only stay one night and be gone the next morning. But one night was all it took. In all of those years of church, of Sunday school, of Bible classes, of reading and studying devotionals, of worship, of mission trips, no one had ever told me the truth about sin—that *it is fun!* Or at least it seems fun at the time before the consequences catch up.

I took one bite of that forbidden chocolate and discovered the secret that had been kept from me my whole life. Sin is *fun*! And there is the Eve factor—choosing sin is empowering. It makes you feel free; it makes you feel alive; it makes you feel invincible, untouchable, in control, and on top of the world! And therein lies the problem: this is a fallen world. This world belongs to evil. And when you are on top of this world, watch out. It's a long, hard fall back to reality.

If you play, you must pay. And the price for me was almost too costly to bear.

Chapter 9

Never Say Never

"I remember Christian and I agreeing that divorce would never be an option."
—Scarlett Rose

A s I reflect on my childhood years and my years as a teenager, it's clear to me that the pattern of our forefathers' sins so often becomes the roadmap of our own desperate behavior. The Bible even speaks on this in Nehemiah (9:16–28). It's as if no matter how hard we try to avoid the pitfalls of our lineage, no matter how determined we are *not* to do whatever it is our parents did, we still slip and fall into the same flesh-driven behavior.

I remember when I was a young girl, and I learned of my father's affairs on my mother. I swore to myself I would never cheat on my spouse. I knew without a shadow of a doubt that would never even be an option for me. I grew into a strong, confident Christian young woman, and I had seen firsthand the heartache adultery brought to both of my parents and to our family. I just knew that would not be an avenue I would ever walk down.

I worked very hard to not drink, gossip, do drugs, or sleep around. Every decision to do or not do something in my youth was a calculated effort to divorce-proof my home. I was mission-driven to break the pattern of broken homes that seemed to plague my family lineage. And somehow it worked back then.

The temptation to do drugs, drink, or sleep around seemed not to even exist in my world as a teen. I let my friends know that even if they decided to take part in those things, I would not. They respected that, and even though many friends made different choices, I was never ridiculed for my abstinence. I had tunnel vision—focused on family, God, and doing the right thing. I know my mother also prayed consistently for my sister and me. Her prayers played a large part in my clean walk as a young lady.

I hadn't worked so hard for this perfect record for nothing! I was determined to find someone with similar morals, like-minded values, and the same clean slate . . . or I would do without. He would have to be someone with a solid Christian family that was together, not divorced like mine. After all, I hadn't saved myself for just anyone. I knew if I ever married he would have to be some kind of special. This would be the perfect formula for a divorce-proof marriage. I needed to ensure that my marriage would not turn out like my parents'. I had it all figured out. Or so I thought.

When I met Christian Robert, I remember thinking I had found the man that I thought didn't exist. And I was not in the least bit concerned about ever being tempted to cheat on him. It just wasn't an option. He was perfect in my eyes, and I was crazy for him. In fact, I remember Christian and I agreeing that divorce would never be an option.

Chapter 10

Mississippi Memories

"The smallest ounce of hope can create the
largest ocean of dreams."
—Scarlett Rose

Christian was from a small farming town in Mississippi, and I was from the big Southern metropolis of Nashville. We both attended a Christian university in Arkansas with roughly four thousand other students.

I remember the day when some friends introduced me to Christian Robert in the library on campus. When I first met him, I was not the least bit interested in dating him. He just wasn't my type, and I didn't find him attractive. He had a sweet innocence about him that was such a turn off to me. He was smart, clean-cut, quiet, and too "All American" for my taste. I normally went after the more alternative, confident types. But, over the course of a short few weeks, Christian started hanging out with me and a small group of other friends quite regularly. In fact, we even named our group "The Posse."

After a couple of months of hanging out, we all became very close. I remember hugs and laughs, shoulder massages, and back scratches. We were an affectionate group, but none of us were dating yet. Eventually, something sparked between a guy and a girl, and they began dating. One of the guys decided to go off to the service, and one of the girls started hanging with another group of girls. So there were four of us remaining, and since two of those were dating, Christian and I ended up hanging out just the two of us . . . a lot.

During this time alone we began to have more in-depth conversations. We discovered just how different we were from each other, and I think it intrigued us both. I had never met anyone quite like Christian Robert. He was so solid in who he was as a person at such a young age. He was just nineteen and only three months younger than me. He was incredibly smart and college was very easy for him. He rarely had to study but managed to make all As. I, on the other hand, had to study like a madwoman! I was a total class clown in high school and played more spades than anything else. And because of that, I had no idea how to study and ended up flunking the first semester of college. Thankfully I got my grades together and spent more time in the library.

Still, I was a free spirit. I was loud and silly and always after a laugh. Christian was introverted, analytical, and a good listener. I remember him asking me question after question about my family, my childhood, my town, my hobbies, and my hopes for the future. He hung on every word I said like he was memorizing my life story. He had a memory like no one I had ever met. He remembered every detail I told him.

I remember his soft grin as he would listen to me carry on about whatever it was that I was blabbing about. I loved to talk, and he loved to listen. I felt cared about, interested in, and safe with him, something that took me by surprise. I remember wondering how in the world I was becoming drawn to this guy. But I was attracted to him. There was no denying it. He was like no other guy I had ever met, and he broke every belief my parents had instilled in me about boys.

After my father's affairs divided our family, my perception was that you couldn't trust men and that they were just out for themselves. My mom drilled in me and my sister that we needed to get educated so we could take care of ourselves one day, just in case the men we settled down with decided to leave.

She was not very trusting of men . . . and for good reason. Her dad left her mom, her, and her three sisters when she was in high school. He had cheated on her mother for years. Finally, my grandma had had enough, and she divorced him, something very bold for my grandma's generation.

And, as if that emotional scar wasn't deep enough, my father cheated on her. I am not sure how far into the marriage my parents were when the cheating began. They were married for seven years before they had my sister. Then I was born almost three years later. They divorced when I was two. He had a pattern of infidelity and had stopped. But Mom said one of his old girlfriends eventually came back into town, and he fell back into old habits. She finally had enough and divorced him.

My father did not want a divorce. He actually went down front at church and confessed. He wanted another try, but Mom felt like she had given him more than enough chances. He was also not always kind to my mom in their marriage. He tended to be self-focused because he was an only child, spoiled rotten by my Grams.

My Mom was a single mom for nine years before she remarried. She was my superhero. My stepfather was around for a span of nine years. They dated for five years and were married for four before he did a total 180-degree turnaround and left. It was crushing to my Mom and a shock to us all. He simply decided he didn't want to be married anymore and gave up. It was heart-wrenching for us—especially my mom.

All those combined hurts were all she needed to write off men for years. And who could blame her? Needless to say, man-bashing happened in our home at times, and although my Mom never said one ill word about my father to us, I was very distrusting of boys. During our biweekly visits after the divorce, my father reinforced my disbelief in men by telling me that boys were out for only *one thing*. After all, he knew, he used to be a boy, he would say. And he'd cheated on my mother. So in my mind, boys were very selfish. They were takers. And when they had taken all they wanted from you, they left. Or they cheated, and then they left.

So how come Christian Robert didn't seem this way? He was a boy. But he didn't seem selfish. He didn't seem like he was out for only one thing. I was intrigued by him. But to be honest, I felt he was putting on a really good act. No boy could be this caring, this kind, this self-less. In fact, we had been hanging out for months and he hadn't even tried to kiss me. I knew I needed to meet his family to decide if this boy was really as great as he seemed. And I'd get my chance very soon.

Christian took friends to his house for amazing Southern meals once a month. It wasn't long after I met Christian that I too was invited to one of these Mississippi adventures. A group was traveling to Mississippi for the weekend, and I thought, *Why not? It will be a new experience.*

To my surprise . . . it was a blast! Christian's family was so kind and hospitable. I had never seen such a group of jovial family members who seemed to truly enjoy each other's company. And the weirdest thing of all—his parents were still married! I felt like I had walked into an episode of *Leave It to Beaver*. When one family member got up to get something from the kitchen, they made sure to ask if anyone else needed anything.

They played board games in the evening. They worked in the yard together on Saturday, and they worshipped together on Sunday. On the Sunday of my visit, we all went to the local Church of Christ. I remember seeing his parents holding hands in the car on the way to church. I couldn't help but stare. I had never seen that before. They really loved each other, and not just that . . . they *liked* each other. It boggled my mind. It went against what my mom had always told me: Get an education so I could take care of myself in case the man in my life leaves. But Christian's dad didn't leave. He had been married for years, and I could tell he wasn't going anywhere. He was happy.

That Mississippi trip was monumental for me. Two things happened that I will never forget. One, I started to see Christian Robert in a different light. Maybe he really was a great guy. Maybe this boy was the real deal. And two, maybe, just maybe marriage could work. Maybe it could be a lasting and enjoyable thing. And maybe, just maybe I could have one of those types of marriages one day. For me, on that trip, hope was born.

It wasn't long after that trip to Mississippi that I allowed myself to start falling for Christian. He was the one.

I knew he liked me long before I liked him. He made it known and so did his friends. I was very drawn to him because he was so patient and did not crowd or pressure me. We dated throughout the rest of our college years and married almost exactly six months after I graduated. Although our love for one another was strong and genuine, nothing or no one throughout our Christian upbringing prepared us for the marital struggles we would encounter.

Chapter 11

Confessions of a Stay-at-Home Mom

"What captures your attention controls your life."
—**Kare Anderson**, *Harvard Business Review*

Josie Rose is three and a half. The recession is upon us.
Those innocent days of college and meeting Christian seemed centuries away now. I could hardly remember why I had fallen in love with him.

I was engulfed in my new world. It consumed every ounce of me. I felt like a totally different person. Tate and I were suffocating under the stress of the new normal we had created. Balancing two worlds and constantly monitoring them both to make sure they did not collide was exhausting.

I remember when Tate and I could no longer withstand the personal darkness we had created.

There was not a specific day or event that caused the turning point, but more of a constant nagging to tell the truth. I felt God Himself was nudging us to come clean so we could be free from the prison of guilt and shame we had become slaves to. It is difficult to describe how exhausting this lifestyle is, especially as self-proclaimed Christians who are involved in the same church. We really started feeling evil.

It was too much to bear. Tate could see how I was hurting under the stress, and he was stressed too. We finally decided to tell the truth. We had struggled for so long trying to stop seeing each other on our own. We knew it was wrong. We knew this affair was killing us. We had been living a double life for over two years. And it was catching up with both of us. Eating at our insides. Destroying the people we wanted to be. The people we had worked so hard to become so many years before.

Those days of peace and simplicity seemed so far away. We wanted to get back there. Back to reality. Our visits of passion and fun and laughter had turned into grueling discussions of how we could get out of the mess we had made. We wanted to make things right, but had no idea where to start, especially since both of us didn't truly want to stop seeing each other.

It was all so confusing and chaotic mentally, emotionally, and spiritually. What was wrong with us? We thought that if we told the truth to each of our spouses, it would snap us out of this fantasyland we had created. We would wake up and realize what we were losing. We would realize that losing our marriages, our families, and our homes was not worth it.

Of course, we didn't know how they would react. It was Russian Roulette. We knew telling the truth was potentially very dangerous. But either way, it was our only way to complete freedom.

We decided to tell our spouses about the affair on the exact same night, at the exact same time. Tate would sit down with his wife and I would sit down with Christian and we would both tell the truth. We knew it was what God was leading us to do. But we were terrified. It was as if we were handing our lives over to our spouses, not knowing what to expect. *Here, have my life; it's broken anyway.*

I chose to go out to eat with Christian. I told him I needed to talk to him about something so we got a babysitter for the evening and went to a local chain restaurant. I waited until after dinner to tell him. I barely ate a thing. He sensed something was wrong. "So what's on your mind, babe? What did you want to talk to me about?" he said innocently. I told him I'd rather wait till we were in the car to talk, knowing I was about to turn his world upside down. He agreed.

We finished our meal and headed out to the car. I walked as slowly as I could. Each step was getting more and more difficult the closer we got to our vehicle. We were sitting in the car at the restaurant parking lot. I was so nervous I was trembling. I wanted to get it over with, so I blurted out, "Let's just sit here and talk."

It was the hardest conversation I had ever had in all of my thirty-two years. How do you tell your spouse of nearly nine years that you have been having an affair for the past two years? And worst of all, I loved this other man and didn't want to stop seeing him. I was going to be honest. And I was going to be honest about it all.

As I opened my mouth, the words slowly fell out like thick mud. I felt dirty hearing them come out of my mouth. What had I become? How did this happen to me? I had promised myself I would never take this road, yet here I was on it, owning it, and not wanting to leave it. It was as if everything were in slow motion.

Christian turned beat red the way he did when he was embarrassed or angry. He asked who it was, but then said his name before I could. "It's Tate, isn't it?" I nodded in shame.

"I knew it. I knew it was him all along," he said in a low voice, shaking his head back and forth. Maybe we hadn't been as stealthy with our looks and conversations as we'd thought.

He hit the steering wheel firmly with his clenched fists. I jumped. He sat there shaking his head for what seemed like an eternity. He could hardly look at me. I was afraid. In those moments, I no longer felt safe with Christian. He was so distant from me, so distant from the solid man I had fallen in love with thirteen years ago. "Do you love him?" he asked.

"Yes."

He turned his head and gazed into my eyes with a look of pure hurt. Then he turned his eyes from me, staring ahead. "Have you slept with him, Scarlett?" I paused. My heart was beating so hard it felt like it would come out of my chest. I answered with my head hung in shame.

"Yes."

He didn't say much more. I sat silently staring out the window at the city, just wishing I could be anyone but me in that moment, wanting the day to be over. We drove home in silence, knowing that from this night on, our lives would never be the same.

Chapter 12

Swept Under the Rug

*"For all have sinned and fall short
of the glory of God."*

—Romans 3:23

**Sweet Josie is three months from turning four and the
only happy one in our home.**

The Sunday after we told our truth, Christian went
to church alone and requested prayer for our two
families. I had gone to Ohio for the weekend to
stay with a college friend. And Tate's family was not there
either. Christian was naïve in thinking the church would
surround us, help us, and reach out to me in a loving way.
It was the exact opposite. I came unglued when he told
me what he had done, but there was nothing I could do
about it.

Once my sin was known at the church, I went to my
Sunday school leader's home and asked if I could address
our Sunday school class. That request was denied. He and
his wife told me no and that they didn't feel it would be

a good idea. It was comical to me how much they always welcomed my honesty in Sunday school class before they knew of my sin. I know now that honesty, brutal honesty scares people. In fact, it was apparent I wasn't wanted there any longer. My monster truth had been released, and instead of it becoming an opportunity for healing, it was another story swept under the rug.

Is this happening all over the globe? Families finally have the boldness to release their truth only to find that their church family doesn't want to hear it, doesn't know how to handle it, what to say, or what to do in response . . . so they don't do anything. How is this Christ-like in any way?

The problem with this silence for me, the sinner, was it was the worst response anyone could have offered.

I know Christian Robert and I were in complete dismay at the reaction from the church. We thought we would be surrounded, helped, lifted in prayer, and plugged into couples who had experienced what we were going through. If the tools weren't available at our church, we thought they would plug us into another congregation that knew how to help us. But it was quite the opposite. No one called. No one came. Christian went to the elders and literally begged them to reach out to me in love. To call me. To please help our family. Our family was falling apart, but the awkwardness of our situation seemed to outweigh their love for us.

Christian wanted to stay in the marriage and work on it. But I felt he never did any of the work. I was completely consumed with anger over how hard I had been laboring on our marriage alone, angry that no one cared to know about that, angry that I was automatically assumed to be the cause of all of this and labeled a temptress and homewrecker, and in my eyes, it all could have been avoided if he had just listened to me.

He knew I was in a bad place and he was now in "save my family" mode. He knew I needed help and he couldn't reach me. He tried as best he could to get the leaders of our church to help, but they didn't. And in their defense, I believe now that they just didn't know what to do.

But the sad part is, instead of finding help for us, they did nothing. They "thought about us" from afar and hoped we wouldn't come back because it was all too uncomfortable. I now understood why a good friend and confidante had told me, "Don't ever tell." Maybe she was right. Things were so bad we decided to visit other churches while continuing yet another round of counseling. We were dealing with Christian's depression and my rage. The counselor confirmed that Christian had been severely depressed for six out of our nine years of marriage. We were a mess.

One Sunday we went to another church on the other side of town, only to run into our own preacher in the lobby before the service. He was visiting that church because his daughter attended there. We spotted him in the crowd across the lobby, and he saw us. It took our very own preacher a good four minutes to make it over to us. When he finally wandered our way, the only words he had for us were: "Hey, how have y'all been?" He said this cheerfully, as if nothing at all was going on in our lives. Before we could even fully answer him, he patted Christian on the back and told us he had been thinking about us. And as quickly as that, he was gone. It was obvious he only came over because he had to, not because he wanted to.

It was embarrassing, heartbreaking, and nauseating. We never heard from him again, and I wasn't surprised. And it was the worst response I could have received. Satan was having a heyday in my mind, filling it with more lies and more judgment:

Ha! They hate you, Scarlett. They know what a whore you are! That is why they aren't reaching out. You're not worth it. You're not worth their effort. They don't care about you now! See how God's people treat you when you come out with your truth? When you are real with them? They can't handle it. What a joke! It's all a lie, you know? There is no Jesus! There is no love for you! There is no grace! Those people never cared for you or for your family. They only loved you when you fit the mold. So typical of these so-called Christians. What a freaking joke. Just go on and live your life for you! Forget about them! They don't love you; they don't even care enough to pick up the phone or come visit you because you are nothing! Your own preacher isn't even praying for you! He can't even stand to be around you! Look at what you did! Can you even blame them? You whore . . . the world would probably be a better place without you in it. Look at this mess you made! No one will ever love you after this. You are ruined. Tainted. Trash. Just give up now and save yourself from this misery. Just end it. You are worthless anyway.

And those are just some of the thoughts the Great Liar dealt me daily. My enticer was now my accuser. It was a constant battle to keep my head above water. I was sinking fast, and my church family was nowhere in sight. We weren't welcome at our church. No one actually said that to our face, but it was a known and strongly felt reality. No one was calling to see where we were. No one was coming over to check on us. I heard the rumors that were going around. I was "after everyone's husband since I had been there," I was "always flirting," and I had even "complimented a visiting pastor once on his curly hair . . . Can you believe the nerve of her?" It was ridiculous. Ridiculous because I knew me. I knew I had only been with two men my *entire* life. I was a virgin when Christian and I married. The only other man I had ever been with was Tate. Yeah, quite the whore. But it still hurt me deeply. And it still fed into Satan's lies confirming that what he was whispering to me was true.

It blows my mind that some church-going people think that gossiping about others when they are at the lowest point in their lives has no effect on them. Let them have their day in the sun. It will come, and the same people they used to gossip about others will no doubt be talking about them. It's really so sad. It makes me think about the verse, "Jesus wept." I believe Jesus weeps over His people breaking down His own children when what they need is love. When what He taught us was love. His very example, His entire life on this planet, exemplified love. His love was unconditional, nonjudgmental, and it met sinners right where they were. That's how Jesus's love changed even the worst sinners, even the coldest hearts, even the dirtiest individuals . . . not because He told them how terrible they were. *They already knew how terrible they were.* Jesus told them to come as they were. And He loved them with no questions, ultimatum, or price to pay.

To all those out there who attend a church and struggle with gossiping about others, quit or leave the church. You are doing more harm than good. You are no better than the person you are talking about, the adulteress like myself, the man addicted to porn and sleeping around on his wife, the alcoholic, the thief, the child abuser . . . the list goes on. You don't see the plank sticking out of your own eye. You don't realize the damage you do to those you speak about.

My mom taught my sister and me this: "If you don't have anything good to say, don't say anything at all." I understand why that adage is important now. Our words are powerful. We can never take them back once they are out there. Our tongue is the most powerful tool we have.

Let's use it to uplift and encourage our fellow brothers and sisters in Christ!

And if you don't know what to say, say just that. Go to the hurting person. Tell them you don't know what to say, but that you are covering them in prayer and that God knows what they need. At least in that, there is love and you are speaking to them as a person with feelings. You let them know that you see them. You care enough to look them in the eyes, treat them as a child of God, and let them know you are praying. Let them know you are perfectly imperfect, just like they are.

It's called grace. I believe it's the reason we are here on earth. To help one another on this wild journey that can get very tough at times and very confusing. Don't make it more painful for those who are struggling. And goodness, if you feel you are about to implode and you just have to gossip to someone about something, then talk to God about it! He will help you see it differently. He will listen. That way you can get it out, but not in a harmful, hurtful way.

Decide to help each other "get through" the journey, not hinder the journey. We all mess up at times. We all fail. We all have peaks and valleys in life. Let's show love to those who are walking in their own valleys. It will make such a difference in that person's life.

Chapter 13

Rumors

"The thief comes only to steal and kill and destroy;
I have come that they may have life,
and have it to the full."

—John 10:10

I had no idea how many horrible things were going to be said about me. In my mind, I was taking the higher road. I was coming out with my truth, as ugly as it was. I had decided to be honest and seek help. I had been instructed by God to tell the truth. I knew it was the right thing to do. That is what I had always been told, what my very church spoke on all the time. Bring your sin into the light, and it will set you free. I knew I was wrong. I knew the horrible choices I had made. I needed guidance, support, and unconditional Christian love. I needed to be mentored by a woman who had experienced what I was going through, and I needed her to have a tremendous bounce-back story. I needed her to tell me I was going to be okay. I needed hope.

Christian was supporting me the best way he knew how, but he was also very direct in telling me how wrong I was and what I needed to do to make things right. He came across as bossy, which made me shut down. He was ordering me to do this and do that.

I am not sure what people said to him, but in my opinion, he was shunned along with me. No one knew what to do with us.

When I can receive more love and support as a sinner from my local bar than I can my home church, there is a broken system.

When word got around—and it got around fast—I never could have imagined how painful and horrific being a part of a church could be. I no longer fit the mold of the "perfect Christian wife." My family no longer fit the mold of the "perfect Christian family." There was no place for me or my family now. We were broken and hurting, and our church had no need for us. Our situation made people nervous, and we were not welcome. It wasn't spoken, but it was known. The sad part was, we wouldn't want to go back even if we could. It was obvious that was not the place of healing for us. I don't understand how a spiritual hospital can turn away a very sick patient.

In an ironic twist of brotherly love, while our family was practically disowned from the church, Tate's family was surrounded with love and support—from the exact same church and Sunday school class. Tate was taken to several lunches and coffees by several of the men in our Sunday school class. Men opened up to him about their own past physical struggles. Tate's sin was accepted and understood.

Men are physical and need physical love. It was understood that you cannot starve a man physically because it leaves him open to being tempted to step out. Women are emotional and need emotional love. However, if a woman is starved emotionally, she should be able to deal with it and it should not affect her.

Somehow they were able to separate the man from the sin, but for me, as a woman, it was very different. *A woman should know better. A woman is not physical and therefore must be a slut to sleep with another woman's husband.*

I was blamed for the fallout in both families. It was a nightmare. Tate was angered by how they treated us so differently. He knew it took both of us to do what we did . . . not just me. He knew and shared with others that he had pursued me, not the other way around. But it did not make a difference.

I still needed some type of closure, so I went to several people's homes, knocked on their door, and hoped they would talk to me. Two couples and one woman allowed me to come in. One was very preachy, one just listened, and one was very understanding because friends of theirs had experienced a similar situation. I thought it was ridiculous that I had to plead to meet people in their living rooms just to be able to tell my side of the story. I am not saying I deserved better; I was definitely in the wrong.

But I wanted the opportunity to share my heart with the couples who had been closest to us at church. I couldn't bear the thought of them not knowing the truth of my side of the story.

I had never been the brunt of gossip before. But I now understood the analogy of words cutting to the core of you and figuratively ripping your heart out. I now understood how rumors caused some people to consider suicide as an only option. In fact, in the very church where I was raised as a young girl, the preacher committed suicide behind the church building after the eldership found out about several relationships he was having within his own congregation. That preacher had more than likely watched many of his own people in congregations past be labeled, shunned, and torn apart by gossip. I assume he knew all too well what the discovery of his sin would unleash.

I, on the other hand, was still naïve. I had no idea what was to come after my decision to tell the truth. The things people said about me were atrocious. I was labeled a homewrecker. I was treated like I had leprosy. I actually had someone jog away from me in the church preschool parking lot when they saw me—like I was a monster. But one of the worst was a lady who pretended to be my friend. She would call me to console me, and then later I found out she was gathering information to take back to the other church ladies. That cut deep.

In another attempt to gather information about Tate and me, the leaders of our Sunday school class and one other individual invited my best friend at church, Lily, to speak with them one night. She had recently walked through a very difficult time with her own family and assumed they were wanting to check on her and possibly pray with her.

A little over a year ago, Lily had discovered that her husband had been having an affair with someone at work. She had been back and forth with her husband, trying to salvage their relationship. Things were not good. Her own family was victim to another relationship outside of marriage. She had been through that dark place and back. And I was amazed at her ability to love people and forgive their shortcomings. Lily had every reason to turn away from our friendship, but she stood by my side just as I had been by hers through her own storm.

That evening, Lily walked into a drill session. She had no idea the entire intent for the meeting was to find out everything she knew about me and Tate. They bombarded her with question after question: "Did you know this was going on?" "How did this happen?" "When did this start?" "How could you have not noticed this?!" Lily was mortified and in total shock.

"Of course I didn't know!" she rebutted. "Do you honestly think Scarlett would be bragging to me about her and Tate after what I have been through? I had no idea!"

They continued asking questions for what seemed like an eternity. They then strongly encouraged Lily to stop associating with me. They communicated that they could not support her friendship with me.

Thankfully, Lily did not take their advice and remained my best friend. After that meeting, she too felt shunned from the church because of her close association with me. It wasn't long after that Lily decided to find a new church home. I was in utter disbelief at how she was treated because of my sin. There are no words to describe how lowly, unworthy, and dirty this made me feel. I felt my own spiritual home base had slammed the doors on me, my husband, and now my best friend. I have had to work very hard at forgiving those individuals.

In God's eyes, gossip is just as destructive as an affair. There is no sin larger than another. No one sin measures greater than the others. Sin is sin. It kills, steals, and destroys . . . period. And we all fall short. However, when I can receive more love and support as a sinner (and we are all sinners) from my local bar than I can at my home church, there is a broken system.

To all of those who are brave enough to speak your truth, know that the rumors will come. And the rumors will go. They may hurt you, but they will not break you. In fact, they will be a blessing in disguise. The rumors will help you determine who your real friends are. They will make you stronger. They will draw you closer to your Lord and Savior.

He will not leave your side. He will never speak one ill word about you, even when you deserve it. He will love you through it. He will hate the sin and the hurt it has brought to your life, but He will love you, the person. He will love you the very same as if you never sinned. Now.

Always. And forever. God IS love. And He is constant. He will always be love.

Rumors will teach you that. Don't be afraid of them. Welcome them. And then turn them over to God.

> *"For every minute you are angry,*
> *you lose 60 seconds of happiness."*
> **—Ralph Waldo Emerson**

Chapter 14

Sierra

"Trust in the Lord and do good."
—Psalm 37:3

Josie is ten weeks away from her fourth birthday.

When you go through trials, sometimes help can come in the least expected ways. Although she doesn't know it, a woman named Sierra made a huge difference in my life one day in the hallway of my daughter's preschool.

Sierra was in our home church group. She had been a friend of mine before the truth of my double life was revealed. We often sat with each other at church gatherings, and her sense of humor and mine were similar. We had never hung out together outside of home church or church events, but I always really liked her.

One afternoon while picking up Josie Rose from the church Mother's Day Out program, Sierra stopped me in the hall. We were standing in the very hall where I used to pass Tate on Sunday mornings. Everywhere in that building, I felt tension and awkwardness. I felt as if I were walking into a den of wolves every time I entered that building. I felt the eyes of judgment and disgust on me from the other mothers who had obviously heard the latest gossip. As much as I hated being there, it wasn't fair to Josie to pull her out of the preschool she loved so much. So four times a week at drop-off and pickup on Tuesdays and Thursdays, I would enter that building and face the awkwardness for Josie's sake. Looking back, I would enter a thousand awkward rooms to live an example of authenticity for my daughter. Not all areas of life are pretty, and sometimes you have to put on your big girl pants and face the music.

Not all areas of life are pretty.
Sometimes you have to put on your
big girl pants and face the music.

But on this particular afternoon while picking up my daughter, Sierra pulled me aside. She looked me straight in the eyes and told me she loved me. She told me she was angry with me. And that she felt betrayed, confused, and disappointed. *But she told me.* She took the time to look me in the eyes and acknowledge me as a sister in Christ, tell me that she was angry at me, that she was hurt, and so very disappointed in me. She told me it may take her a while to process all of this. And that she may not speak to me for a while, but that she would be praying for me and Christian. She told me that she loved me. And her actions confirmed that she cared enough to talk to me, to see me, to acknowledge me as a person, not as my sin. She didn't know the right words—and honestly, there probably weren't any right words—she just knew she needed to tell me her feelings. She cared, and it meant so much.

That moment made me feel like a person again instead of an outcast. It gave me hope that others out there felt like Sierra, even though they might not be able to voice it like she did. It proved Satan a liar. Not everyone hated me. Sierra didn't hate me. She loved me. She cared enough to be disappointed in me and that meant she had expected more of me. That was a great sign. And a boost of encouragement during such a time of despair. I loved her for being honest with me.

Of all the people I knew in that church, of all the ladies I had been in home church with, taught Bible school with, and worshipped with, Sierra was one out of only two women, other than my best friend, who pulled me aside, looked me in the eyes, and treated me like a friend—even after the horrible things I had done. She saw me. She gave me hope. Sierra is a true woman of God. Not perfect. But godly. She was Christ to me when I needed Him most.

Silence does no good. Rumors do no good. Judgment does no good. Labeling does no good. Arguing who is right and who is wrong does no good. Telling someone how bad they screwed up their life does no good. But acknowledging a person in a loving, humble manner and speaking love over them even when they don't deserve it— that does *so much* good. That kind of good changes lives.

Chapter 15

Healing the Wounds,
Not Covering the Scars

"Never, never, never give up."
—**Winston Churchill**

Josie is four and a half years young.

It took me a long time to come to grips with the reality of my situation. I had spun out of control and been selfish for so long that I hadn't stopped to see the destruction around me caused by my own self-serving choices. It was as if I had this hulkish side to me . . . a monster that had lain dormant within for so long and the trigger of neglect and rejection awoke the beast within. I was blinded by my rage from not being heard, not being seen.

When I came to, the ruins of my family were devastating. Not just my own family's hurt, but so many others. It was as if I were surveying the scene after a detonation, with the evidence of shrapnel all around me. My family was ripped apart, and I had caused the explosion.

Christian had moved in with a friend. We were officially separated. Christian's family was in a state of utter dismay. Many had reached out to me, and the discussions were excruciating. I loved and respected his family so much, and I had let them all down. I had brought shame to the family name.

On the other side of town, Tate and his wife were still trying to decide if they could salvage their relationship. He was trying to do the right thing for his three kids. His wife wanted to make it work, but she was devastated. Tate was all she knew. They had dated since high school and had literally grown up together. I'm sure she couldn't imagine life without him. She refused to speak with me or acknowledge any form of communication. I couldn't blame her. I reached out via e-mail, apologizing for hurting her family and telling her that I never meant to cause pain to her or their children. She did not respond, but I got word that she interpreted the e-mail all wrong and felt I was digging the knife even deeper.

It seemed wherever I made an effort to apologize or own my poor choices, it backfired in my face. I could do nothing right. I was a screw-up, a failure. I was continually told I had "ruined my life" and "ruined my daughter's life." I lost friends left and right. I lost many Mary Kay customers because a lot of my customer base was from church.

Even family members looked at me differently. I felt my own mother couldn't look at me at times, she was so disappointed in me. That pain alone cut to my core. My mother was my hero, my spiritual mentor. She taught me about Jesus. She took me to church. And now I had done the same unspeakable thing to my husband that my father had done to her—the thing I swore I'd never do. If my own mother had given up on me, how could I heal and be okay after *this*?

**I had a choice every day.
Keep moving forward or quit.**

The affair now defined my life. It was as if wherever I went everyone knew and looked down on me in pity and shame. I started to mope like Eeyore around my home, unable to do simple tasks like fix my daughter's lunch for preschool, and I knew she could tell something was very wrong. Everything I attempted to do was hard, and it was as if everything moved in slow motion. The days were so long and taxing. I felt a heavy dark cloud of guilt and shame hovering over me at all times. And the cloud got more cumbersome with each passing day. My heart literally ached. It was a pain I could not explain, but it physically ached constantly. I wanted to ease the torment and heal my heart like you would a stomachache or a headache, but there is no Tylenol for a broken heart. There is no quick fix.

This pain was all new to me. This must be the reason God Himself commanded, "Do not commit adultery." I knew now the why behind the "do not's." God was trying to protect me . . . protect me from this agony.

How did this happen? How did I become so angry, so blinded by my emotions that I would not stop to think about the repercussions of my choices? Hadn't I been taught my whole life to live for others? To put myself last? To do the "right" thing no matter what? I knew better. I knew right from wrong. I knew God. So how could this have happened? How could God let me get so far off course? Why hadn't He saved me from me?

I would hear from Tate now and then. He was worried about me, but we agreed talking during this time only confused things. I respected his choice to work on his family and gave him his space. But I missed him dearly. He had become my best friend.

Christian reached out every day, multiple times a day. It felt like borderline harassment, but looking back he was just trying to salvage our family. I can see that now, but in the midst of the despair, I was so consumed with anger that I loathed him for it. He wouldn't listen to me three years ago when I was begging for him to go to counseling, begging for his attention, but now he wanted to talk about our relationship multiple times a day? It was too much. Too late.

Before the affair had started, friends of ours at church had announced they were getting a divorce. Christian and I were completely blindsided by this, but they admitted they had been struggling for some time and the husband admitted to having an affair. I remember telling Christian, "If it can happen to them, it can happen to us. This scares me. Something is not right here, we need counseling." But then the next day there was nothing—no conversation or acknowledgment that I'd had a concern. Another discussion had and forgotten, pushed under the rug. Looking back to those days infuriated me. Why didn't he listen? Why? All of this could have been avoided! I was haunted by all of our past conversations and all of my pleading. My thoughts of those days kept swirling around in my head, and it only increased the bitterness in my heart.

It felt as if I were stuck inside a nightmare. Every night when I went to sleep I would hope that when I woke up, everything would be back to normal and I would realize this was all a bad dream. But each morning I woke up to the ugly truth. To my fresh wounds. To my battle scene. I had a choice every day . . . keep moving forward, or quit.

But quitting was not an option because of my precious Josie. So every day I woke up. I put my feet on the floor. I took a deep breath. I lifted up my chin, and I decided to live for my daughter. She made me want to do better. She made me want to try harder. She made me want to figure out just how I got where I was, so I would never end up back here again. She made me want to heal my wounds, not cover the scars.

I knew covering the scars would only mean passing my shame and guilt from my own bad choices onto her, and I refused to let that happen. I wanted my sweet girl to have every freedom in every decision without an emotional attachment or negative attitude from my own mistakes and failures. I knew it was a long road ahead. But a journey of ten thousand steps starts with one. I was on a mission to find victory and to free my daughter of this family pattern of guilt, shame, fear, and failed relationships. I didn't know how it would be done . . . but I knew it had to be done.

> "Do not worry about tomorrow,
> for tomorrow will worry about itself.
> Each day has enough trouble of its own."
>
> **—Matthew 6:34**

Chapter 16

Embrace

"What's done is done."

—Rosa Belle

Sweet Josie Rose was named after my Grams. Josie was soon to be five.

My Grams was my confidante. I knew whatever I told her stayed between us. She was my soul buddy, as we called it. When I looked at Grams, I knew I was looking at myself in sixty years. She was such a spit-fire, full of life and spunk. She was remembered everywhere she went. She never understood why, but I did. She was pure sunshine bottled up in a tiny four-foot, ten-inch frame. A force to be reckoned with, my Grams.

So why do I tell you about my Grams, Rosa Belle? Well, I used to talk to her about everything. And she would just sit and listen. Rarely did she comment on my situations or life happenings. She just listened. Never did I feel judged or less-than in her presence. She always accepted me as I was.

She had loved my father through so many poor choices. She stood by his side—even through the ugliest of times. Not taking up for him, just loving him. "Wrong is wrong," she would always say. I've never known anyone else like my Grams, and I am so honored to have known her. I carry her with me wherever I go, and I try to show the same unconditional love to my daughter that she always gave to my father and me.

One afternoon I went to visit Grams in her assisted living home way out in the country. She didn't necessarily like being so far from us, but she liked this retirement home better than any of the others we had tried. The attendants were kind country folk, and boy, could they cook. I sat by Grams's side that day and started to talk to her about the mess I was in. She knew about Tate, and she knew I had told the truth about my affair. As I sat crying over the fallout from my situation, Grams sat still and calm. When I finished pouring out my heart and asked for her guidance, she simply said these words to me: "What's done is done."

She was right. I had made my choices, and now I was paying the consequences. It surprised me that those simple words resonated so strongly in my spirit. It called attention to my new reality. What was done was done. I couldn't change it. I couldn't wish it away. I could only make good choices from that point forward and make lemonade out of my lemons.

Grams's words often pop into my head. They have helped me on many occasions. When I start to slip into my analysis-paralysis, I think about Grams. I can choose to wallow in thoughts of "Why me?" and play the victim, or I can own my choices. I can embrace my imperfections. I can choose to make my mess a message and live from here.

> *"God grant me the serenity to accept the things I cannot change; courage to change the things I can; and wisdom to know the difference."*
> —**Reinhold Niebuhr, "The Serenity Prayer"**

Chapter 17

Broken

"For I know the plans I have for you," declares the
LORD, *"plans to prosper you and not to harm you,*
plans to give you hope and a future."
—Jeremiah 29:11

Josie Rose is a whole handful, and five years old.

Our marriage did not survive. I think the final straw occurred while we were out of town visiting some college friends. I always kept a journal. It was my private place. My place to pour out my heart, which was a difficult thing for me to do. But in the pages of my journal, I felt safe knowing I was the only one who read it. I was writing about me, for me.

During these months of being without Tate, my journal had become the place I vented. I went there to talk about Tate and my feelings for him. I needed a release and a place to process what I was feeling. It was a way for me to dump my emotions and be able to move on. I never intended for anyone to see my journals—ever. And these journals were my thoughts and various feelings at various times. They were not decisions or necessarily the path my actions would take. It was simply a safe place to say and express whatever I was feeling. In all of my different counseling experiences and workshops on self-improvement and healing, they always encouraged journaling. It had become my sanity. My sanctuary. It never once crossed my mind that Christian would read it.

My girlfriend, Jen, and I went out that Saturday afternoon to a local consignment shop and to lunch. I desperately needed girl time, and Jen was like family to me. Her home in Ohio had become my refuge. When we returned from lunch, I remember Christian acting very distant and almost cold with me. I didn't read much into it, but on the ride home, he began drilling me with questions related to facts and information that only I knew about. I took a deep breath and calmly asked, "Did you read my journal, Christian?" He sat in silence as he stared ahead, driving down the freeway. "Did you?" I asked again with more frustration in my tone. He didn't speak a word but cut his eyes over to me as if to say, *I know it all now.*

I was appalled! I felt as if he had violated my heart and raped my soul and my innermost thoughts! Who was he to even touch my journal!? I had never felt so invaded in my life. My safe place had been broken into, robbed, swarmed. It was in that moment that any and all trust I had rebuilt with Christian over the past months was destroyed. I couldn't trust this man. My childhood beliefs came flooding back to me. He had no idea who I was.

If he had a *clue* about who I was as a person, he would have known that was the *last* thing he should have done. I could not forgive him for taking my safe place from me. So much had been stripped of me—not *this too*!

For a brief moment of silence, I reflected on how Christian must have felt the night I told him about my affair. So much trust had been broken between us. We had hurt one another so deeply. In my mind, I was taking the fallout for our marriage. No one knew how hard I had worked to reach Christian. No one knew about his deep depression and emotional absence. No one cared to know. It was easier to lay blame. Easier to point the finger. I was to blame for it all. Now the only place I could go where there was no judgment was gone.

It was too much for me to take at the time. I despised him for not listening in years past. I detested him for saying he cared *now*, wanted me *now* and would work *now*. Why didn't he show up *then*? Before my name was destroyed.

At that moment, in my mind . . . I knew I was done. We argued for a solid hour on that ride home and then there was only silence. It wasn't long after that trip that we agreed to divorce. I had zero desire to work on anything with him, and he had read enough of my journal that I am sure the words haunted him.

He wanted to file, and I didn't care who did it. I was beat, exhausted on so many levels. Christian and I divorced a few months shy of our tenth anniversary. I lost. I lost my family. I lost my husband. I lost my job as a stay-at-home mom. And I lost my innocence.

We lost. We lost our marriage. We lost our family unit. And we lost our innocence.

Josie lost too. She lost her family. She lost the gift of watching us grow in love for one another in years to come. She lost the joy of knowing how it feels to have one home. She lost the security of knowing her parents are united in a mutual commitment. She lost the wisdom and insight of our reconciliation. And worst of all, she lost so much time with both of us. Her daddy was now across town and she was lucky to see him a few times a week. Josie lost her mommy to a job that had to pay the bills that my new single-mom life demanded.

No one wins in divorce except Satan. Everyone loses. And in my opinion, it doesn't solve your problems; it only births a new set of complications.

I had been divorced for only a couple of months. It was one of the most painful, emotional processes I had endured so far in life. It was as if Christian had passed away, yet I would still see him from time to time when he came to visit Josie. It was an exhausting time psychologically, emotionally, spiritually, and even physically. Going through our things and deciding who got what was awful. We were, however, cordial with one another for the most part.

Christian let me keep most of the furniture because a lot of it was antiques given to us by my Grams. I believe he also wanted to keep things as normal as possible for Josie inside her home. We argued a lot, especially about debt, but we never cursed at each other or name-called. I remember one evening, a discussion escalated into a yelling match. Ugly things were said to one another in a hateful, raised tone. We had never yelled at each other before. I stopped this out-of-the-ordinary, loud, mean-spirited conflict and told Christian, "Even in this, we are better than talking to one another that way." He agreed, and from that day forward I do not remember us raising our voices or name-calling ever again. Even in our brokenness, our character remained intact.

Josie Rose did surprisingly well with the transition. I guess in her mind not much had changed, and maybe it felt like her daddy was just working a lot like he had to do at certain seasons. She was as sweet as ever and very affectionate. She loved us both so much and was such a happy little girl. You never would have known her parents weren't together anymore.

She had finished out her three-year-old preschool class at our old church, and Christian and I decided it was time for a new school. She had been attending a small Baptist preschool down the road from our rental house, since we had sold our home in the fall of the previous year. There was a small sense of peace in not having to walk through that grueling process along with everything else.

I managed to find a part-time job with my degree in marketing at an IT firm across town. My schedule aligned perfectly with Josie's new preschool schedule. My metamorphosis into becoming a single mom was probably as smooth as it could have been. I can look back and see

God's hand on our situation and on our hearts, even amidst our divorce.

Tate and I would check on each other from time to time. He knew about my divorce, but he had decided to try and work on his marriage a little longer. Things had been very tough, he reported, but we did not go into details about his situation. It was for the best.

I was a wreck emotionally. I felt so alone and isolated in my new life. I had never had my own place. I wasn't used to being alone. I had transitioned from my adolescent days at my mom's house, to college, to my sister's for a bit, and then to marriage with Christian. Now I was alone. Alone with my thoughts. I wasn't used to it, and I hated it. I felt tormented by my past and the collapse of me, the me I used to love.

I was crying out to God on my knees in my bedroom one evening, wailing and begging God to help me survive this new life I had to live. I needed guidance. I needed strength. I needed the courage to face each day. Thankfully, Josie was with her dad for our new every-other-weekend rotation. Although we had shared her during our separation, she was gone for longer periods of time now. Her being gone overnight was only two months new to me. It was terrible being without her. I felt like my heart would leave every other weekend.

My heart also hurt so deeply over what I had done. The shame and guilt seemed to weigh on me heavier than anything I had ever experienced, and I missed Josie so much that it felt like my heart had been physically removed from my body and no one cared to bandage my wound. It was almost too much to bear. I remember God whispering these gentle words to me that night with such calm confidence: "It's okay. It's okay."

I remember arguing with Him in my mind as I continued to wail. *Okay? This is not okay! I am not okay! I am a wreck! A hot mess! Look at me, God! Do I look okay?!* I remember hearing the words again and again in my head until I started to calm down. I stopped arguing with God and started listening to this steady, repetitive message, "It's okay. It's okay," until my spirit settled. I began to repeat the words out loud to myself. The more I heard them, the more they felt comfortable and hypnotizing. At first, I muttered them through my tears. "It's okay. It's okay." Very soft and not convincing at first, but slowly I spoke them louder and louder with more confidence. "It's okay. It's okay." I began nodding in agreement with my Lord. "It's okay. It's okay," until I had completely steadied myself. I didn't understand how this mess I made was going to be "okay." But I knew God had given me these words.

I knew He understood my pain. I knew He would not lie to me. I knew He wouldn't leave my side. I was angry at God at times. But then I always knew my pain was a result of my own choices. God didn't make me sleep with Tate. I chose that. Still, God could help me through the pain.

My faith grew through all of this. I honestly felt like all I had to lean on for strength was my faith. Tate was gone. My mom was emotionally gone. Josie was too young to lean on. Christian was gone. And his family was gone. It was just me and God, so I couldn't stay mad at Him long. I read my Bible almost every night—the same scriptures over and over. I closely identified with the story of the woman caught in adultery, and I read those verses every night before I fell asleep. Some nights it was the only way I was able to sleep.

Somehow, someday it would all be okay, even though at the moment I had no clue how I would get there.

…but Jesus went to the Mount of Olives.

At dawn he appeared again in the temple courts, where all the people gathered around him, and he sat down to teach them. The teachers of the law and the Pharisees brought in a woman caught in adultery. They made her stand before the group and said to Jesus, "Teacher, this woman was caught in the act of adultery. In the Law Moses commanded us to stone such women. Now what do you say?" They were using this question as a trap, in order to have a basis for accusing him.

But Jesus bent down and started to write on the ground with his finger. When they kept on questioning him, he straightened up and said to them, "Let any one of you who is without sin be the first to throw a stone at her." Again he stooped down and wrote on the ground.

At this, those who heard began to go away one at a time, the older ones first, until only Jesus was left, with the woman still standing there. Jesus straightened up and asked her, "Woman, where are they? Has no one condemned you?"

"No one, sir," she said.

"Then neither do I condemn you," Jesus declared. "Go now and leave your life of sin."

John 8:1–11 (NIV)

Chapter 18

Learning to Lose Like a Winner

"Your attitude determines your altitude."

—A Zig Ziglar belief

Josie is six and a half years old.

There is an art to losing. Maybe you have never thought of it that way, but it's true. When I was young and played little league softball, my coaches would refer to it as good sportsmanship. We were not allowed to make ugly faces or comments to another team if they beat us. If we did, we lost our concession treat after the game. In fact, after each game, both teams would line up and walk past each player on the opposing team and say, "Good game, good game, good game," while high-fiving the other team's players.

There is a way to lose like a loser—and there is a way to lose like a winner. Anyone can win like a winner and lose like a loser, but it takes someone with self-discipline and superb character to lose like a winner.

Every day when I put my feet on the floor and got out of bed, I had to decide if I was going to lose like a winner or lose like a loser. I'd like to say every day I chose the latter, but that isn't true. There were days I was plum worn out and grumpy, knee-deep in self-pity.

I discovered losing like a winner is especially challenging when you lose something dear to your heart. It's one thing to lose a softball game like a winner, and it's totally different to lose your family like a winner. I can say this for certain—the days I gave into my mopey loser attitude were the toughest days. Everything seemed so much harder, so much more difficult, and so much more tiring on those days. The days I kept it together and chose to lose with my chin up were better days. Not easy, but better. I've learned faith makes things possible, not easy.

> *"I can do all **things through [Christ]**
> **who gives me strength.**"*
> —Philippians 4:13 (NIV, emphasis added)

I'll never forget the first time Christian Robert took another woman on a trip to Disney World. Disney had always been a very special place for us when we were together. We went there on our honeymoon, and we had an amazing time. We also took our mothers there three years later. I remember Christian and I talking about how that was probably the last time we would be at Disney alone as a couple, and that the next time we came we would have children. We guessed right, and the third trip to Disney was with Christian, Josie Rose, and my mother. Josie was two months from turning five.

The truth had come out about my affair one year prior, and Christian and I would be divorcing in one short month after the trip. Despite our circumstance, however, we both felt strongly that we wanted to take our daughter to Disney together for the first time. Neither one of us wanted the other to miss out on the experience with her. So we made it work. It was an awkward trip, but a good trip nonetheless. Three separate times Christian and I were able to visit Disney and make beautifully different memories there. Shortly after our Disney trip, we were able to tell Josie about the impending divorce.

Josie was told in a way that was emotionally appropriate for her. We explained to her that Mommy and Daddy would be living under different roofs and that we loved each other, but that we got along better when we didn't live together. She never questioned it until she was older.

Three years later, Christian told me he was taking Josie and his girlfriend at the time to Disney World. I came unglued. It rocked my world like I never could have imagined. I wailed. I screamed. I ached internally at the thought of this woman bouncing around Disney with my family. It made me feel physically sick.

After the trip, I sat Christian down and let him know how it had destroyed me. I didn't hold back. I told him all the ugly details of how I felt while they were gone. Shortly after, he broke up with that woman. He only said these words: "You learn a lot about someone on a trip."

Looking back on that event, I did not lose like a winner. I pouted like a loser. I transferred my anger and disappointment to Christian. I wanted him to feel the way he had made me feel. I wanted him to know how he ripped my heart out yet again, and how I felt he disrespected the memories of our relationship and family at Disney. I did not want him to enjoy his trip. I did not want him to have freedom in that place to make new memories. I did not want him to win. I wanted him to lose as big as I was losing, if not bigger.

Fast-forward a couple of years and Josie, her father, and his newest girlfriend of about a year took a trip to, you guessed it, Disney World. I will not lie—I still felt anger. I still hated the thought of some strange woman sleeping in the same room with my family. I loathed the thought of her experiencing Disney with my daughter. Riding rides and laughing and making memories with my Josie while I was back home, missing her and going to work like any other day. It wasn't fair. It still hurt my heart. *Why Disney? Why does he always have to go there?* I would think to myself. I woke some nights so angry I couldn't fall back to sleep. I was shocked that after almost five years of being divorced, this trip still affected me this way.

The fact is, it will hurt when your ex moves on. Unless you are a coldhearted snake, it will cut deep like nothing you have ever experienced before. It will turn your world on its end, but you will live. The sun will still rise. Your heart will still beat. Breath will still fill your lungs. Life will go on. And you will have a choice to make. Do I pout and lose like a loser? Or do I keep my chin lifted and lose like a winner?

Many, many tears were shed during the eight days my sweet Josie was on her trip with her daddy. But she will never know. She will only know a guilt-free enjoyment to live her life to the fullest whether she is with her daddy or me. I choose to love her father from afar, support him as best I can, not because it is easy, because it is what is best for Josie. And because I believe that is what God would want of me.

Christian Robert and I both made poor choices, but why should our daughter continue to suffer from them? I truly believe that the better I treat her dad, the more love Josie will be able to experience in her heart. The more security she will feel. And the more well-rounded and emotionally healthy she will be. Now, that is something to be thankful for. That is losing like a winner!

I choose to lose like a winner. Count my blessings in the now. And be thankful for the good times I did have when we were married. Today I choose to focus on my daughter and what is best for her. I choose to take me out of the equation, and support her father and respect his choices. In the wise words of Dr. Seuss, "Don't be sad it's over, be glad it happened."

On the days I chose this attitude, I realized there is so much to gain in losing. Again, I wish I could say I chose this attitude every day. But I did not.

Some days, however, opportunities arose that felt like they were heaven-sent.

Chapter 19

The Power of Saying "I'm Sorry"

"The first to apologize is the bravest.
The first to forgive is the strongest.
The first to forget is the happiest."

—Anonymous

Sweet Josie Rose will soon turn seven.

All three of the ladies seated next to me had been cheated on by their husbands, and as I sat there getting my nails done, I realized one of us was not like the others.

They talked about the other women and what trash they were. They bashed their husbands for all the crap they had put them through. They bashed the two-bit whores who had slept with their husbands and had shown no remorse. They carried on about how stupid these men and their mistresses were. They called the women horrible names, and as I sat there I realized they might as well be talking about me! I had been "the other woman" . . . but I wasn't trash. And I most certainly wasn't a whore.

I knew in that moment I had a choice to make—either keep my mouth shut and shake my head silently as if I agreed with them. Or, perhaps I could give them a different perspective.

I felt the stirring in my spirit and I could not be silent. I spoke up. "Well, I have actually been the other woman." An awkward silence fell over the small group of three women as they looked at me. They had been so brazen seconds earlier, and now they were dumbstruck.

I confessed that I was lost and hurting. That my husband was almost like a robot, unable to be reached and empty of emotion. That I felt so neglected and alone and unheard, and that it made me temporarily insane. I talked about how I had only been with my husband before Tate and that I was a good, God-fearing woman—a Christian woman who loved her family—but rebelled. I told them he wouldn't listen to my words so I spoke through my actions. It was almost like a call for help that went south. Way south.

Not a single woman moved, let alone spoke. I told them how remorseful I was. I told them that I had tried many times to reach out to Tate's wife, now ex-wife, to tell her how sorry I was for all the hurt I caused her.

I knew from their conversation that the quietest most introverted of the three was also the most recently abandoned, having been left for the *other woman*. She sat looking at me in utter disbelief, perhaps that I had spoken up and admitted that I had been *that* woman. She finally spoke up—the lady whom her husband left her for was his secretary at work. She said she had known this woman for years and that they had been friends. She told me that now this woman will not even look at her or acknowledge her. She said she felt so betrayed by both of them. And worst of all, she had learned about the affair from her twelve-year-old son.

There was so much pain and defeat in her eyes. Her words struck to the core of my being like an emotional lightning bolt. *I had done that.* I had done that to Tate's wife.

Grief overcame me. Shame sank in my stomach like a wet towel, and I couldn't refrain from apologizing to this woman. There, in the middle of the nail salon, words flowed out of my mouth like poetry, almost as if God Himself gave them to me.

I looked her in the eyes and said, "I have never been able to apologize to the man's wife who I had my affair with, but I can apologize to you. I am so sorry for the hurt that I caused. I had no justification for my actions. They were selfish and destructive and senseless. I was wrong. And I am so, so sorry for all the hurt I have caused."

A wave of heaviness lifted from her eyes. Tears began to fill where heaviness once was. She smiled a soft gentle smile and said, "You are awesome."

That day I witnessed the power of saying, "I'm sorry," and I believe two hearts healed a little bit more in that moment.

"Every time you are tempted to react in the same old way, ask if you want to be a prisoner of the past or a pioneer of the future."

—Deepak Chopra

Chapter 20

Crack in My Barrel

*"Fear is just a bunch of lies
keeping you from your purpose."*
—**Scarlett Rose**

Josie is seven years old.

Christian and I decided to meet at Cracker Barrel. God only knows how many times we had dined there as a family and with in-laws and friends from church over the years. Christian said he wanted to talk, and I agreed and told him to name the place and time. The time was now; the place was Cracker Barrel.

Christian and I spoke just about every day. We always knew what was going on with each other's schedule, and we were helpful to each other as needed. We both agreed that our friendship and helpful attitudes created the best environment for Josie. He would often joke about me taking him back. "Return to your best friend," he would jest in an e-mail. I kept a collection of e-mails when he had casually mentioned giving him another chance. Christian joked a lot, and sometimes it was hard to know when he was being serious. But when he asked if we could sit down and talk, it felt like this conversation was going to be different.

It was shortly after Christian's trip to Disney World with his first girlfriend and Josie Rose. Our sweet Girlie was in second grade at the time and thriving; she had a cheerful spirit and such a positive attitude. Everyone at school doted on her. They had even nicknamed her Sunshine. It was a tough year for Josie academically because the teacher she had been assigned was previously a fourth-grade teacher who was now teaching seven-year-olds. She was all business and learning without much friendly fun, unlike Josie's previous teachers.

Despite the divorce, Christian Robert and I parented well together, and we both were very involved in her schooling and extracurricular activities. She had studied Irish step dancing, was playing the flute, and was also playing softball. She seemed to be a natural at whatever she tried. We were both so proud of our little Rose, knowing that she was the one thing we did well together.

On the other end of the spectrum, Tate and Vicky had gotten divorced. Tate and I dated off and on throughout the years and broke it off so many times that we both lost count. The guilt of how we began put a damper on our relationship. We were unsure if we could make our relationship work simply because of how it began. I tried to date others during our break ups, but I always ended back up with Tate.

Now face-to-face over a basket of biscuits, Christian and I were seated at a small two-top by the wall. We sat and chatted for a bit about work and our families, just catching up on the latest. Then I asked him, "So, what's up? What did you want to talk about?" I was usually the one to dive right into the deep conversations; Christian had a history of being more of the avoider.

Christian looked at me almost as if he was struggling internally to find the words. He paused, took a deep breath, and then stated that he knew now why I had left him and understood why I would never want to try things with him again. He admitted to me that he had not been a good husband. He wanted to let me know that he would try again if I was willing and that it would be totally different this time.

This conversation took me by surprise. I sat there almost in utter disbelief that he was taking any kind of ownership of his part in our failed marriage. He had always been so quick to blame the affair and Tate for everything, and often declared that I had never given him a chance.

I sat looking him in the eyes and then down at the table and then back to his eyes, not really knowing what to say. Tears started to seep. *Don't cry. Don't cry*, I kept thinking to myself.

I had always loved Christian. I had never stopped. But it felt like the man I married had disappeared. I prayed almost daily that he would find himself again and find his smile again. Deep in my heart, I missed my Christian Robert . . . the one I had been so crazy for in college . . .

the one who challenged everything I had been taught as a child about men and marriage . . . the Christian I hadn't seen in years and didn't know if I would ever see again.

My mind was whirling, trying to compose a response that made some kind of sense. But at that moment, nothing made sense. How could two people go through what we had gone through, sit across from each other casually discussing our own marital demise, and yet be smiling at one another with an awkward care and concern for the other? Christian continued to mystify me. This was not what I had expected.

I wanted to get up and run out of that restaurant. I wanted to take off to a place far, far away where no one knew me or what I had done. I wanted a fresh start, a clean slate. I was so tired of battling the what-ifs in my mind and the must-haves. But I knew I couldn't leave; I couldn't run. There was Josie Rose, my sweet angel girl God had given me. Maybe God knew in His infinite wisdom that if He hadn't blessed us with Josie, conversations like these would not have occurred. God knew I would have run without her . . . and I never would have truly healed.

Of course I doubted what he was saying. Christian always seemed to know what to say to me to keep me on the hook just one more week or one more month. He was a planner and not always a doer. I still did not trust him with my heart. No way. The risk was too great to take.

I finally opened my mouth and thanked Christian for sharing what he had. I knew it was hard for him to open up. I then continued to tell him that I did love him and that I was thankful that we had salvaged our friendship somehow through the mess we had made. I told him how good Josie was doing and how I thought it would hurt her terribly if we tried and it didn't work.

Readers who have been through divorce will understand. It's hard to put into words just how excruciating a divorce is. We had finally reached a good point in our current relationship and situation. He was dating again and I was with Tate. Josie was doing well. Why would I risk all of that and Josie's heart for a what-if?

Although I did love him still, I was afraid I wasn't *in love* with him. Yes, I loved him as the father of my child. I loved the Christian I met years ago and hoped he would return one day. But I had not seen that Christian in years. I was pessimistic about ever seeing the man I fell in love with again.

At the time, I felt I was protecting Josie from the heartbreak of knowing her father and I were together and then having that taken away. I didn't think I could survive it again, and I didn't want Josie to be subjected to that heart hurt. After all, she didn't even remember Christian and me together. I had a "Let's be thankful for what we have" mentality, and I didn't want to risk anymore heartache. In reality, I was projecting my own childhood feelings onto Josie.

I told Christian that he would find someone whose only desire was to be a homemaker and cook and tend to the domestics instead of an extroverted adventurer. I was not your average homemaker and had never been, despite his attempts to make me that way. He disagreed and said he knew now what he wanted in a woman, and that he wanted a mix of both.

Instead of feeling happy about that, I took offense to it because that was what *he had* in me—what he hadn't appreciated before.

Tears began to form in his eyes. He already knew my answer.

After a few more minutes, our meeting ended cordially. I thanked him for talking to me and he thanked me for meeting with him. He made a point to say that if I ever changed my mind he would be there. And that was that.

As I got into my car, I cried at the weight of it all. I cried out of anger and frustration. I cried because I missed the man I fell in love with. I cried because this was all too difficult.

After pulling myself together, I remember thinking to myself that he would never find another woman like me. Looking back, it was arrogant of me to think that. And I was wrong.

Chapter 21

Like Sands Through the Hour Glass

"Time really does fly."
—Moms everywhere

Josie is nine years old.

Life carried on. I was still employed at the IT firm across town but had gotten promoted to business development. I thrived in my new position and adored being out and about selling instead of in the office. God had prospered me, and I was able to afford nice things. I had so much confidence as an independent single working mom. I continued to grow in my faith at my new church. I had been working with the kids' program there for four years now. I loved how my new church taught me how to live life to the fullest and how to be a better mom, a better friend, a better employee, a better daughter, and a better me. Every lesson from my pastor was a message I could apply to my daily life. I was learning how to forgive myself finally and how to enjoy life again.

Josie was also thriving. Ball games, tournaments, graduations, trips, church, recitals—you name it, we were up to our eyeballs in it. As Americans, we tend to run around like chickens with our heads cut off trying to keep up with our children's activities. We rush from here to there, from there to here, trying to remember to eat in between events and games and school and work and life. We try so hard to fit it all in, afraid our kids are going to miss out on an opportunity or a moment.

Meanwhile, we are snapping photos and zipping out posts on social media so everyone knows how happy we are and how much we love our kids and how we obviously have it all together. Ahhh . . . the American dream. Before you know it, you turn around and years have passed and you wonder, *Where did the time go?* It's all a blur of fast-food meals, hustle and bustle, and road rage. You begin to ask yourself, *Was I present for all those moments that flew by too fast? Did I soak it up enough?* To all those ladies who stopped me when Josie Rose was a sweet baby and encouraged me to enjoy every moment, you were right . . . time really does fly.

Christian and I continued to get along. So much so that most people didn't know we were divorced until we told them. In fact, we got along better than most married couples. It was comical to us, but we preferred friendship. And we were grateful we could cheer for Josie side by side. I had read somewhere that if you can sit in the same vicinity as your ex at your child's ball games, it was easier on the child if they hit a home run or made a good play. That way they wouldn't have to choose which parent to look at or run to when they celebrated their victories. It made sense to us.

Christian was dating someone new and had been for a little over a year. I was still with Tate, even though we had broken it off a number of times over the years, taking a few months here and several months there. He and his wife divorced seven months after Christian and I had. We had a lot of shame and guilt to work through, and we both spent a lot of time on the counselor couch.

I still had cobweb corners of my heart that God knew needed cleaning out. He loved me too much to leave those dark forgotten corners untouched.

He was now a different man, and I was a different woman from the people we were when we met years ago. We had both worked very hard on ourselves to determine what each of us had brought into our previous relationship that had added to their demise. We agreed that it took two to make a marriage work and it took two to break a marriage. We owned our mistakes and decided to become better people instead of bitter people. We agreed that if the other had been the same person they were years ago when our affair began, we would not be dating each other today. We had truly changed from the inside out—for the better. People can learn from their mistakes and change.

In fact, I believe that not only can people change, but they can become even *better* people after large failures. God's Word is saturated with stories of people who failed hugely and then He used them to grow His kingdom and reach the broken.

I read once that it isn't the success of an individual that makes him or her great, it's how high they bounce back after failing. I like to call it bounce-back-ability. Tate and I both had bounce-back-ability, and we both understood just how difficult a climb it was after being so low. We admired that in each other.

Even though I never shared it with Christian, deep down in my spirit I still had hope for my family. I would find myself at times daydreaming of one happy home, one Christmas, one schedule, and the simplicity of life before my divorce.

Tate and I talked about everything, and we discussed this topic occasionally. We both missed the simplicity of life before the divorce. He missed his children tremendously, and I hated splitting up my time with Josie. We agreed it was probably a normal feeling and dismissed it. I had never been divorced and didn't know how it was supposed to feel. So I just kept rocking along with life, surviving and striving to be a good mom to Josie and a loyal woman to Tate. But somewhere deep inside, I still felt responsible for Christian. I still cared about his well-being. I still loved him. I just never acted on it out of fear.

In fact, I buried it. I didn't feel worthy of Christian all those years ago when I met him at college, and I certainly didn't feel worthy of him now after what I had done.

I felt *even* with Tate. I felt we were on the same playing field. He understood me and what I had been through and how hard I had worked. And I understood him. We talked. We listened. We cried. We worked. We never gave up on each other. We respected one another. I loved Tate and he loved me. I was honest with Tate, and I wasn't afraid to tell him how I felt. He knew I missed my family unit because he missed his as well. And Tate knew I still loved Christian, just as I knew he still loved his ex-wife, Vicky. The affair didn't change the type of people we are. We have big hearts. We care. We are compassionate. We knew we had hurt them both. We knew we had hurt each other.

It was a tough pill to swallow, but we carried it every day and used the tools we had learned in therapy to manage the guilt and emotional aftermath of our choices. I felt strong in who I was and in my relationship with Tate. But I still had cobweb corners of my heart that God knew needed cleaning out. He loved me too much to leave those dark, forgotten corners untouched.

Chapter 22

Cobweb Corners

"If God wants to teach you a lesson, He will.
It's up to us how many times we walk through
the same storm until we finally get it."
—**Scarlett Rose**

Josie is just three months shy of her tenth birthday.

It was a normal Saturday like any other. I had been divorced for almost five years now and was completely used to our every-other-weekend schedule. Josie was at her dad's house that weekend and was probably hiking or doing something fun with her dad and his new girlfriend, Rachel.

Rachel had become a part of Josie's weekends at her dad's. I wasn't sure what to think of it, really. It was a weird feeling for me, but like many feelings connected with Christian, I pushed them away. Tate was busy with his son's soccer game, and I was at home cleaning house and doing laundry.

As a single working momma, Saturdays alone became my catch-up day after a busy workweek. I remember walking through my hallway on the way to get a load of laundry from the washer to move over to the drier when I heard God's gentle voice in my spirit: "Talk to him."

I immediately stopped dead in my tracks and started questioning God with a child-like, belligerent attitude. *Talk to him? Seriously? Why do I always have to do the talking? Why now?*

I knew exactly who God wanted me to talk to. I was scared. I was angry. I was proud. I didn't want to talk to Christian! I wanted to keep going along as I had been. I wanted it to be life as usual. He had his life. I had mine. We had our setup, and it worked just fine. I had my feelings, which I kept to myself, and I liked that.

I don't want to talk to him! I won't. No. I don't want to!

I battled with God in my mind, knowing He heard me loud and clear. But in His simple, calming wisdom, He spoke again: "Talk to him. Time is running out." I sank slowly to my knees, defeated. I knew in my spirit He was right. Of course, He was. He was I Am. I wept and sobbed and wept some more.

"I'm scared, God . . . I'm scared," I barely squeaked out through my tears. *I don't want to. I don't want to. I don't want to.*

But I knew I had to. I'd never won an argument with God yet, and my fights with Him were getting shorter. "Okay, Lord. Okay," I muttered aloud, surrendered and frightened.

I called Christian a few minutes later and asked him to meet me at a local restaurant that next Monday for lunch. "We need to talk," I told him.

Chapter 23

Egg in My Eye

"Do not be anxious about anything, but in every situation, by prayer and petition, with thanksgiving, present your requests to God. And the peace of God, which transcends all understanding, will guard your hearts and your minds in Christ Jesus."

—Philippians 4:6–7

We decided to meet at the Egg and I. It was a fairly new restaurant in between where we both worked and I had not been there yet. As I drove to the restaurant, my palms began to sweat and my stomach was in a mass of knots. This was going to be interesting. Christian had no idea what I was calling him to talk about. He had tried to get me to tell him the reason for the meeting on the phone, but I had not alluded to anything. What was I supposed to say? "Hey, umm, I changed my mind. I want to see if we can get back together and restore our family after being divorced for five years." This was all so weird. But I trusted God, and in His infinite wisdom, I knew this would all work out according to His plan.

I always felt like Christian and I would somehow make it back to one another. So I guess I thought this was how it would all go down. This was how God would orchestrate our reconciliation and redeem our love story. A conversation over tea, a decision, a switch would be flipped. We were going to do this. It was what was best. It was the only way this whole mess could ever end up okay, right, and good. I just had to find my words.

I prayed the entire car ride to meet him. I spoke scriptures out loud for encouragement. "I can do all things through Christ who strengthens me." "The joy of the Lord is my strength." I had the local Christian radio station on for positive background music. I needed all the help I could get. What in the world was I going to say?

Okay, God, this is Your show. Please give me the words. Please.

I felt stupid. I felt vulnerable. And because this had happened so quickly, I felt like I was betraying Tate since he had no idea about the conversation about to take place. I felt so many different things. I felt excited. I felt terrified. I never knew I could feel so many different ways at one time.

I pulled into the parking lot five minutes early. *Wow*, I thought to myself. *That never happens.* I sat there trying to breathe and checking my makeup.

Oh shoot, I hope I wore the waterproof mascara this morning. Don't cry. Don't cry. Don't cry. Be strong. Be strong. Be strong.

I was trying to pump myself up to get out of the car and start walking toward the building . . . but my rear was glued to the seat. Two minutes and counting. What was Christian going to think? Maybe this would be no big deal. I would pour out my heart, he would say, "Thank you but no thank you," as I did to him the last time we had a "talk," and I would leave and go about life as usual. Yes, maybe that was all that would happen. Quick. Easy. Business. Done. I could check off that I talked to Christian, done and done, and go about my merry way.

Okay. Let's do this.

I peeled myself off the leather seat, stood up, shut the door, and started walking.

Doing good. One step in front of the other. You've got this. Breathe. Don't forget to breathe.

As I approached the restaurant, I didn't see Christian anywhere. He was never late. Never. I stood outside the Egg and I waiting. *Could he not do it? Could he not sit across from me and talk? Maybe he changed his mind? Maybe it was all too weird? A random call out of the blue about needing to talk after all these years . . . maybe he just didn't care to talk to me.* Things had been different now that he was with Rachel. He didn't call and chat as much as he used to. I could tell he was content with her. *So maybe that's why he will stand me up. Maybe he just . . . Oh. There he is.*

I looked up, and Christian was walking right toward me. He had on khakis and a plaid button-down dress shirt, his typical work attire. He looked very nervous. In fact, he may have been more nervous than I was. When he got closer, I greeted him and poked fun at him for running late to lighten the mood. I asked him how he was. He said he was okay and anxious to hear what this was all about. He didn't look too good. His face was flush and he looked like he could throw up at any moment. I'm sure I looked close to the same, if not worse. Our poor waitress was about to have a winning table.

The hostess seated us at a two-top close to a window. I was facing the restaurant and Christian was facing the window. I tried to make some small talk at first. His answers were very short and to the point, and he finally spoke up and asked, "So, what is all this about, Scarlett? What did you want to talk to me about?"

Crap, I thought to myself. *Can't we just keep talking about nothing?* I'm sure I had a deer-in-the-headlights look when I opened my mouth to speak.

"Well, it's just that God put it on my heart to talk to you. Well, He kinda told me to talk to you. And so here I am. And . . . well, I am so thankful that we have been able to become friends after all we have been through. It's a miracle, really. Ya know?"

He was listening intently and nodded in agreement. His face was puzzled, anticipating the meat of the conversation. I was jittery and continued struggling to find the words. "We have both worked hard on ourselves and to be better parents for Josie. I just want you to know that for years I have tried to not love you. I didn't want to love you. I was so angry at you for neglecting me and rejecting me and not listening to me and not going to counseling with me. I was just so angry that you blamed it all on me and on the affair when I know if you had just listened and gone to counseling with me, none of this would have happened, and even though I have not wanted to love you, Christian—even though I have pushed it away for years and years—it just won't go away. Dang it. It just won't.

"I *do* love you. I have always loved you, and as I watch Josie growing up so fast I just want the best for her, you know? I want her to have siblings and a family and see a marriage that works. I want her to see the best of us. And I have not shown her my best. I don't know how you feel, but I want her to see us at our best together. I want to show her that a marriage can work and that it can go bad and get good again. I want her to know that I love you and how great a dad I think you are.

"I want so much for her. I want the very best. I am not sure what I am saying. I just know I needed to tell you that I have loved you all these years, and I wish I could go back and make different choices, but I can't. This is where we are.

"I want you to know that I am willing to change paths if you are. I don't know how it is with Rachel or where you are, but Tate and I are good. We are really good. He is wonderful, and I do love him so much and we have the relationship I always wanted with you, but . . . he isn't Josie's dad and he isn't the one I committed my life to.

"I have thought so much about all the work that Tate and I have had to do together. So much work. And I think about how it would be if I had poured that into my family . . . Where would we be now? Would Josie have a brother or sister? Would we be stronger than ever? I don't know. I just know that it's work either way. And I am starting to want to be married again . . . and wanting a family again . . . and if I know it takes all this work, why not pour that into my own family, my first family?

"I'm not sure what I'm saying. I just know God told me I needed to let you know I think these things. And that I have loved you all this time, but I was too stubborn and too fearful of the unknown to tell you."

After what felt like ten minutes without taking a breath, I stopped talking. I had just opened Pandora's Box and dumped it on the table. I sat dumbfounded at what had just come out of me, what must've all been hidden in the darkest corners of my heart.

I sat and waited for Christian's response. It was the longest twenty seconds of my life. And then he spoke.

Chapter 24

The Handshake

"Life begins at the end of your comfort zone."
—Neale Donald Walsch

He grinned at me ever so slightly. Christian was afraid of me. I was sure of it. Why shouldn't he be? I had betrayed him, broken his spirit, crushed his ego, and now I was asking if he wanted to work on things because God told me to talk to him. What a crazy loon he must've been thinking I was.

But in a typical calm, Christian style, he said these simple words: "I'd love to try again."

I was still in shock from what I'd just said and now I was in shock at his answer. Had he just said what I thought he said?

He smiled hesitantly and continued to talk to me about Rachel and his relationship with her. It was good, he admitted, and she was wonderful, but he missed Josie and the family unit. He admitted he had always loved me, too, but he had convinced himself he could be happily married to someone else. He had always wanted to try, but I had never been willing when he was, and vice versa.

He joked about us heading to the courthouse right then to lighten the mood. I laughed, and we casually decided to shake hands, symbolizing that we would do whatever it took to put our family back together. We both agreed it was what was best for Josie.

He praised me for my courage to talk to him about this, and then in an unexpected move, he stated he would break up with Rachel that night, assuming I'd do the same with Tate. That caught me way off guard! I was thinking we would digest our conversation for a day or two, and then talk with Rachel and Tate in our own time.

Then it hit me. Tate. My baby. Sweet Tate, who had been so patient, so supportive, so present for me for so many years. We wept together over our mistakes and over missing our children and losing our families. He was my companion. He would be so confused and hurt and angry. *Oh, Lord, now what? Do I need to break up with Tate tonight?* Dear me, I hadn't thought past step one: Talk to Christian. I went from relief to overload in a matter of minutes.

Christian and I left the restaurant feeling much different from when we had arrived. It was done. I talked to him. And it felt good that I opened up. It felt nice to be vulnerable and share what had been suppressed for so many years . . . but the reality of my next few days began to overwhelm me before I even got back in the car.

I knew exactly what God was referring to when He said, "Talk to him." However, I had no idea what

Christian's response would be. Sure, I knew that leaving Tate was a possibility, but I really hadn't thought past the initial conversation with Christian.

How would I tell Tate that Christian and I were going to work on things? I climbed back into my car praising God for how well that had gone and begging Him to speak to me again. *Dear Lord, give me strength for the next step.*

Chapter 25

One Step Forward, Two Steps Back

*"I never knew how capable I was
of hurting so many people."*
—Scarlett Rose

The very next night was the eve of my birthday, and Tate had planned a dinner date for us. I was late from work that evening and met him at a steak restaurant after taking Josie to my mom's while Tate and I went out. I pulled my car into the parking space beside his Charger and took my time getting out. I was nervous. How was I going to make it through dinner without letting on that something was terribly wrong? Tate and I didn't keep secrets from each other. We knew each other too well, and just like reading a book, we could usually tell when something was up. Maybe that came from going through so much crap together.

As I entered the steak house, he greeted me with a huge smile and a big hug and told me how happy he was to see me. To be honest, I am not sure what I said. The whole meal was a blur of warm chatter and trying to avoid any serious conversations at the table. When the waitress asked us if we wanted dessert, I said, "No thanks" before she even fully finished her question. I was ready to leave and get this over with. *What is he going to think? What will I say?*

We walked out to our cars, and Tate asked me to join him in his vehicle. I opened the door, and there, sitting on the passenger seat, was a beautiful miniature rose bush with two greeting cards beside it. "HAPPY BIRTHDAY, BABY!" Tate exclaimed.

"Awe, baby. Thank you. You shouldn't have."

You really shouldn't have . . . Oh my stars, this man is so sweet to me. Tate was a romantic. He loved surprising me and put a great deal of thought and effort into his surprises. He was the best gift-giver I knew. I was really going to miss that. *I am really going to miss him.*

"Baby, I need to talk to you."

"You do? Well, don't you want to open your cards first?" he said. So I did. One was super sweet about growing old together and showed an elderly couple dancing in the kitchen. The other was just silly and good for a laugh . . . but I didn't laugh. In fact, I started to cry. "What's the matter, honey?" Tate asked, puzzled. "What is it? You don't like the card?" Tate was always trying to get a laugh or a smile out of me. I grinned through my tears.

"The cards are great. You're great. I love you, you know?"

"I know you do, baby. What is it? You haven't been yourself all night? Did your mom say something about us going out?" Tate knew my mother still did not approve of him or our relationship. It was something I had battled in my mind for years. Her approval was so important to me, yet she did not know Tate well enough to make a true evaluation of who he was. She had labeled him from the beginning and had never given him a chance. I understood where her dislike came from, but I knew who Tate was. I knew he was a different man, a generous man, a humble man, a great man with a heart for God.

"No, sweetie, she didn't say anything. It's just . . . It's just. Well . . . you know how we always said if there was ever an inkling that we would tell the other."

I could see the utter disbelief in Tate's eyes. He leaned forward, shaking his head back and forth, not believing what he was hearing. I had a flashback to the night I told Christian about Tate; it instantly made me nauseous. But Tate and I had made a pact years ago: if either of us at any time had even an *inkling* to work on our family or our marriage, we must tell the other and the other would step completely out of the way.

He was visibly angry. "Why now? It's been years, Scarlett, years! We've come so far and overcome so much and now this? I don't understand."

"I don't understand either, Tate. I really don't. You know I never stopped loving Christian. You know I miss my family and I want what is best for Josie, Tate. She is my priority. And I have told you that if God tells me to do something, it is God over you every time. I'm sorry. I'm so, so sorry. God told me to talk to Christian and I did, and we are going to try to make it work. I'm so sorry. I don't want to hurt you. I just want what's best for Josie Rose. You know I love you so much."

"It's your choice, Scarlett. Not God's. God gives us free will. You are forgiven. For the love of all things good, Scarlett! Why can't you just let it go? You can't fix what happened! You can't. It happened. You are a good woman and a great mother. Josie is doing great. She's great. You're great. We're great. Life is good. Why are you doing this? It doesn't make sense."

"Tate, please. Please don't make this harder than it already is. God told me to talk to him and I did. I can't go against God. I won't. I have an inkling. It was our pact. I am honoring our pact. We are always honest with each other; that's who we are. I'm just being honest, Tate."

He sat there dumbfounded with tears in his eyes. He knew when I made up my mind it was made. There was sadness, confusion, and disbelief in his expression. He turned his lips in together the way he always did when he was frustrated about something. "Okay, Scarlett. Well, I wish you the best. I just don't know if I will be here for you if this doesn't work out with him. I can't keep subjecting myself to this back and forth and back and forth. It's too hard on me. I love you, but it's just too hard."

"I love you, Tate Rogers. And I get it. Can I have a hug good-bye?"

I put on a good tough-girl front, something I learned as a young child. My dad always told me to suck it up and that crying was a weakness. I still battled with being able to cry in front of others.

We stepped out of his car and embraced in the headlights. Tate had already closed himself off to me. I could feel it. Before he let go, he told me not to call him, not to text, and not to come by. He was going to give me what I asked for. He kissed my forehead, got into his car, and pulled off into the night. I looked up into the night sky wondering if God was looking down on me. Did He see me? Did He know how difficult all of this was? Tears started flowing. Instantly I felt an emptiness in my heart.

What had I done? I never knew how capable I was of hurting so many people.

God, You had better have a plan in all of this, I thought as I drove home.

Chapter 26

Winds of Change

"If it doesn't challenge you, it won't change you."
—Anonymous

Our Little Rose will be ten in two short months.

It had been three weeks since my birthday, and it was like everything had been flipped over. Christian and I turned both of our worlds upside down. We were awkward and out of sorts. When Christian broke the news to Rachel that we were going to work on our family, she was angry—*livid* might be a better word—and marched out of his house with all of her belongings. Who could blame her? Just like with Tate, things in their relationship were also going great and this news had come out of left field. Christian didn't give much detail, but I could tell it was hard on him just by his eyes. Rachel was a good woman, and she didn't deserve this. I felt the same about how I had hurt Tate. I think the only reason we were able to do it was because we felt it was for the greater good. It was best for Josie.

Christian had been coming over in the evenings now and spending more time with Josie. I could tell little Rose liked having her daddy over. I remember watching them throw the softball in the yard one night. I sat on the steps of my porch, enjoying them play together . . . then an old, familiar feeling came back to me. It was the same feeling I used to get when I would watch Tate play with Josie early on. It was an odd, "something isn't right" feeling. I knew I had that feeling because Tate was not Josie's dad . . . and it was strange seeing her with a different man. Now the tables had turned. I was so used to seeing Tate throw the ball with Josie that all of a sudden, it seemed like Tate should be out there, not Christian. It was so weird. Christian was her daddy, but Tate had become the man in Josie's life at our house. I wondered if Christian had similar feelings when I was interacting with our daughter. Did he see Rachel there in his mind? I remember shaking off that feeling quickly and then scolding myself for even thinking such things.

Christian caught me gazing off deep in thought. I was looking his direction but looking through him. I noticed him looking at me, and I smiled a small smile at him, to thank him for being here. He smiled back acceptingly. I was proud of the parents we had each worked and prayed to become. Josie was an amazing girl.

I had done a lot of reflecting over the course of these three weeks. In the evenings I would cry a lot. I ached for Tate, but deep down I knew I was doing what God had instructed me to do. I would sit in my tub and sob. I submitted my will to God. It was difficult but good. I could feel my flesh fighting it. The humanity in me still wanted control, but for the first time in my life, I was fully relying on God. I had prayed for five years for His guidance, His wisdom, and His understanding of the heart. Now that I had time to sit and listen, it was as if He spoke to my spirit directly. Maybe all this time I just needed to sit and listen. The chatter of my own plans, my own wants, my own activities, my TV shows, my social media, my thoughts of how I believed things should be were all quieted. I turned it all off. I went from being addicted to distraction to wanting complete silence. I wanted to only hear from God. I was in His Word daily, seeking and memorizing. Growing my arsenal. I went from thinking I knew it all and feeling in complete control to understanding I knew nothing and surrendering. I felt empty of knowing anything, but it was okay. I was ready to listen and learn. I would have a question, and God would reveal His insight almost as if He whispered it to my heart.

God revealed Himself to me in bold ways. He called me out on my pride and on my arrogance. He showed me that no one on earth can redeem themselves through their own deeds or through the superficial approval of others. He called me out on my addiction to people-pleasing. He made me realize I was capable of unconditional love, the same love that for years I believed I didn't have in me because of my dysfunctional background. He blacked out Satan's lies in my life as if He had gone through the book of my personal thoughts with a Sharpie.

Everything felt so different walking with God and walking in His plan. *I should have done this years ago*, I remember thinking to myself. I was totally trusting God and believing what I could not see. And He held my hand the whole way. Amidst the chaos of my emotions and the stormy changes of this season, God was my calming reassurance. With each passing day, I had no idea how all this would play out. I only knew I had to lean on my Lord because I missed Tate so much. It was as if my heart had been cut in half. As dramatic as it sounds, that's how it felt. And in a strange way, I believe Christian felt that way about Rachel. He didn't talk about it, of course, but I could tell he really missed her. He wasn't smiling and joking as much as he used to. We were very quiet around each other. In fact, we were quieter than we normally were as friends.

I survived the days, and most of my evenings were filled with tears. Christian and I had created our own separate lives over the last five years, and no matter how much we still cared for the other, it was awkward trying to bring those worlds back together.

In our fourth week of trying, the oddest thing happened. God put Rachel on my heart several days in a row. I would be at work and she would pop into my head. I would be driving and—*boom*—a thought of her would surface. The weird thing was, I had never met this lady. I hadn't the slightest idea what she looked like or really who she was other than her occupation. Nevertheless, she was on my heart, and I knew God was placing her there.

Finally, I called out to God, "What?! What do You want now?" and He whispered back softly to my heart, "Talk to him about her." At this point, I was mystified. Completely and utterly mystified.

You want me to talk to him about her? *After I just talked to him about us and our family? You cannot be serious, Lord!*

This was making me angry. What kind of psychopath would Christian think I was? We shook hands on this. It was a done deal. No matter how hard this was, we had made a decision.

"Talk to him," the voice said again. I knew it was God. And I knew what He wanted. And it made no sense.

This is Your grand plan? No! No, I won't. I won't. I need a sign. Not unless You give me a sign. I battled with God in my mind. I was consumed with frustration and confusion.

Within minutes, my phone dinged. I looked at it and saw a text from Christian. "Do you think we made the right choice?"

I could not believe my eyes! Did I just read what I thought I read? Christian never second-guessed anything. For years he had wanted a chance to make things right. For years he flooded my inbox with take-me-backs and return-to-your-best-friend messages.

This was blowing my mind. This was my sign. I texted him back and asked if he could come over to talk at my house later that night. At 9:00 p.m., we would talk . . . again.

Chapter 27

Clenched Fist

*"Sometimes love means letting go when
you want to hold on tighter."*
—**Melissa Marr**

I was straightening my living room like a madwoman. If someone didn't know me, they would have thought I was on drugs. I cleaned when I got anxious. So I was cleaning up until I heard the knock. Christian was on my front porch knocking softly so he wouldn't wake Josie Rose. My house was a small three-bedroom, two-bath starter home. It had been perfect for Josie and me over the years and I was proud I was able to buy this home on my own after my divorce, but quiet was hard to do in our humble abode. I walked to the door very hesitant and unsure of exactly what I would say. I was once again leaning on God to give me the words. *Oh, God, give me Your words . . . this was Your idea.*

I opened the door. "Hey. Come on in."

I had bought a brand-new couch and a comfy, oversized chair for my birthday the year before. It was across the room from the matching gray couch. Christian greeted me and plopped down in the chair. I took my place on one of the couches. We were both as nervous as middle school kids on a first date. "So, what's up?" he asked. Christian's face was turning red. I wasn't sure if it was his nerves or if he was angry at me for calling yet another meeting to talk. To be honest, I was beginning to get on my own nerves with these talks.

"Well, I just needed to talk to you. You see . . . God has really been calling me out on some things . . . It's crazy, really. It's like I've taken a crash course in spiritual and emotional healing or something . . ."

I giggled awkwardly, trying to break the tension, but Christian wasn't laughing.

"It's just that all these years I have wanted my family back together, and I wanted to make it all right and prove to everyone that I am a good person and that good, God-fearing people do stupid, self-serving things sometimes, but that doesn't make us bad or tainted. It just makes us human.

"God has really shown me that it doesn't matter that I screwed up big-time. He has shown me grace and shown me that everything I did is on the cross. The price is paid. I am truly free if I'll just accept the gift and stop trying to save the world all by myself. I guess what I am saying is . . . I love you, Christian Robert. I have loved you ever since that trip to Mississippi. I never stopped loving you. I just was too darn proud to show you or to act on it or to go to you. I was so angry. I was so tired of everyone blaming me. I wanted you to hurt as bad as I hurt when you left me for TV and sports and worrying about money and being out with your friends and always choosing other people and other things over me. You cheated on me too, you know? Anyway, I let all of that anger and resentment and disappointment drive my choices.

"And here we sit, five-plus years later, and I realize you don't owe me anything. And I don't owe you anything. And I don't owe my mom anything, or Tate anything, or Vicky anything, or anyone anything. Because Jesus paid it all. I get it now. I get grace. I get it. And I want you to know that you don't owe me a thing, Christian.

"I'm not sure what you have been going through these past few weeks, but I do know that God has put Rachel on my heart. And it's totally weird because I don't even know this woman, but she has been all over my heart. If you are missing her and if you love her, you should go to her, Christian. It's okay. Josie will be okay."

His eyes immediately filled with tears. He had been listening intently while holding the collar of his shirt to his mouth in a nervous fashion.

"Have you been missing her? Do you love her?"

More tears were filling his eyes and as one would fall, he would catch it quickly with his shirt collar. He nodded hesitantly and then spoke. "I think I screwed up a good thing. I jumped in too hastily. I . . . I was just so excited about the thought of all three of us being back together. I do love you, Scarlett. Please know that I do."

I immediately jumped off the couch and sat at his side. "Christian, you didn't screw it up. Don't you see? God is using me to tell you to go to her. I love you too, Christian, and I know you love me. *I know.* I just think we have never let each other go. I've never let you go. I was so scared to . . . but I want you to be happy more than anything. And because of that I know I am able to love the way I thought I never could. I love you unconditionally, Christian.

"I want you to be happy, and if you are missing her, go to her. Tell her that you made a mistake. I promise you it will be okay. God has put her on my heart. It isn't too late." He was still too choked up to respond.

"All those years we were married, I wanted you to fight for me. To choose me. And now Rachel wants you to choose her, Christian. I just know it. Go to her. It isn't too late."

Christian sat and stared at me through his watery eyes. His hand still held his shirt collar against his mouth. His eyes seemed to turn a shade darker to a deep blue, and he gazed at me with a serious look. Then he dropped his collar from his mouth. "I meant everything I said." I nodded and a tear slid down my cheek. I knew he was referring to our talk at the Egg and I restaurant. "I love you, Scarlett, and I will always love you." Then he agreed he had never let me go as well. We both decided it was time to let the other go and that in that, we were loving each other the best way we could.

He stood up. Then I stood up. We embraced, both shedding more tears—tears of finality, closed doors, and new chapters. He pulled away and in simple Christian Robert form said, "I'm glad we had this talk." And with that, he turned and walked out of my love life forever.

As I shut the door, I felt God's power leave me and the flesh take over. I slid down the door, weak from what had just happened, overwhelmed with grief. I had let him go. I encouraged him to go. So why did it hurt so bad? I cried and cried and cried some more. My safety net was gone. It was just as I had feared. I was scared to death.

Tate was gone. Christian was gone. It was just me and God. And He wasn't done with my cobweb corners yet.

Chapter 28

The Catalyst

"There are two types of pain in this world:
Pain that hurts you and pain that changes you."
—Anonymous

I wish I could say that I woke up the next morning chipper and cleansed of Christian. But it wasn't that way. I experienced heartache that I never imagined in my wildest dreams I would ever have to endure. This was death—the death of my hope for a family reunited. And I would have to mourn it or be consumed.

Coming from a dysfunctional family background, I never really even planned on getting married. In my mind, if I never married I would never have to go through a divorce. In my family, marriage meant eventual divorce. My grandparents on my father's side were the only couple I had witnessed who had stayed together, and as much as I loved them, they argued constantly.

I reminisced about how I had gotten to this place in life—a working single mom with a record of a failed marriage and a twice-broken heart from that marriage. I recalled in college how all that I believed about marriage was challenged after meeting Christian Robert. As I thought about the last twenty-four hours, I realized I never really believed in marriage, but I believed in Christian and felt that with him I would be safe and we would somehow be magically protected from the threat of a split home.

My memories shot back to those early days. I remembered feeling so confident about our uniting in holy matrimony. I literally had zero doubt in my mind on the day we wed; I was so incredibly happy. I remembered how hard we worked to stay true to our Christian beliefs and how we waited to be with one another until that day. I also remember feeling invincible in our early years of marriage.

Funny how that sounded now . . . I had been divorced for nearly six years and Christian was now choosing another woman over me—for good. It felt like a second divorce in my heart. I was breaking up with the fantasy of Christian and me reuniting, and I was losing hope for reconciling my family.

Six months later, I nearly lost hope in life altogether.

I received a text from Christian one early December afternoon just six months after we had attempted to reunite our family unit. We still texted each other daily, and when my phone dinged and I saw his name, I figured it was another inquiry about Josie, her school work, or her schedule. But instead, he requested I come by his place because he had something to share with me face-to-face. He only allowed for a fifteen-minute visit before I would need to pick up Josie from basketball practice. I knew then that this was not a normal conversation. And I knew in my gut what he was going to be telling me. Still, I agreed to come by.

Rachel had taken him back after that excruciating night when he left my house in tears, afraid that he'd lost her. They had been dating for almost two years. He seemed happy again. He had found his smile and conquered his depression. He was running again, something he hadn't done since college, despite my many attempts to get him off the couch during our years together. He was taking care of himself and had lost over thirty pounds. I was proud of him.

I was terrified of what he was going to say this afternoon. On the drive over, my stomach sank. I prayed almost continually from the moment I read that text until stepping onto his doorstep that evening. "I can do all things through Christ who strengthens me. I can do all things through Christ who strengthens me." I repeated Philippians 4:13 over and over and over out loud, encouraging myself as my current pastor had taught me.

I took a deep breath and knocked on his front door softly, not really wanting him to open it. He answered the door and greeted me warmly with a guarded smile. And I knew.

He was nervous. I was anxious. I had so many questions, so many things I wanted to say, but instead, I just listened. He reminded me that awhile back he had agreed to talk to me face-to-face if ever he and Rachel decided to marry. And then he continued by stating, "That time has come."

As I sat there on his couch, the same couch that was once my wedding gift, I stared at the wall ahead, searching for the right words. An awkward silence fell over the room. Then, through my tears, still staring straight ahead at the wall in an attempt to keep it together, I told him that I was happy for him—I paused to catch my breath—but that I was also sad. It was a difficult talk for us both.

"So, do you have a date set?" I asked sheepishly, not really knowing if I wanted to hear it or not. "It will be soon, sometime after the holidays. We've talked about the fourteenth," he replied. *That's less than four weeks away . . .* I remember counting the weeks up in my mind.

We continued to talk for the next ten minutes. We both agreed that in our years together we had done our best to take care of each other with the tools we had at the time. I made him promise that he would be emotionally available to this woman, that he would work hard at this marriage, and that if Rachel ever breathed a word about going to counseling he would go with her. He said that he would.

At that moment, all I could think of was my sweet Josie. I didn't want her living through another divorce. I hardly knew Rachel. I had only met her one time. I was dumbfounded that this was happening. It all felt like an out-of-body experience.

I guess deep down I never thought Christian would remarry. I just couldn't envision it for either of us unless it was our own reuniting. We had become such good friends. We lived around the corner from one another and attended every event of Josie's, usually sitting together or standing in the same vicinity. We had created a family that was not ideal, but it was a close Plan B. Our family wasn't under the same roof, but it was still comfortable and loving and supportive and we got along. I felt all of this would shrivel up and die the moment he pledged his life to another woman. In fact, it was one of the reasons I had not married Tate. I believed it would change the dynamic of our situation. Christian and I would not have been able to be such good friends, sit at events together, do Christmas together, etc. Everything would change if one of us married. But this was out of my control.

Up until now, I had pledged my life to only one man. And I still loved and supported him from a safe distance. I liked our setup. It worked. The thought of this new change threatened the safe world we had created. I was losing control. And Satan was already all over me about how this new marriage would destroy what Christian and I had worked so hard to create for our daughter.

The next few weeks following our conversation were the longest weeks of my life. I was not prepared for the bizarre emotional roller coaster I had just been thrown onto. But Satan—the father of lies—was, and he was strapped in right beside me, yelling his distortion in my ear the whole time. He didn't let up, not once. It is my belief that Satan wanted to derail me from that roller coaster. So far off that *I would never come back.*

I used to be ashamed when I reflected on this low time in my life; it made me feel weak. But now I realize it's another layer of my story that proclaims just how good God is, and that bringing our struggles into the light is actually brave because it helps others who may have struggled or who are struggling in this area. Sometimes when we are in the middle of life's tornados it's impossible to see what God is doing and where He is leading us. We are blinded by the chaos of the storm. Sometimes the things we walk through or the things God asks of us don't make sense until later, when we can view the whole picture.

I want to be transparent with you and share these innermost thoughts with you. Even though it is excruciating to revisit, I feel a deep need in my spirit to share. I believe that it is God's Holy Spirit tugging on my heart, instructing me to share, reaching through my story, through these pages, to connect with you. God loves you so much that He called me to share these moments with you. It was one of the darkest times of my life and the great deceiver's final shot at silencing me forever.

And it nearly worked.

Chapter 29

Ducks in a Row

"Knowledge without action equals greater pain."
—Onsite Counseling Center

Sweet Josie is ten years young.

The grief I experienced in the wake of Christian's news surprised me. I had never known hurt like this—even during and after the divorce. In all my pain before, I always had hope. It fueled me to keep moving forward. I had never been without it. I never knew how powerful hope was until it was gone. I was now in a desert of despair.

I just wanted to sleep. I wanted to stay in bed and rest and not have to face my days. Every morning I would wake up and remember all over again that I no longer had hope. My hope for my family was gone. I struggled to be motivated to shower or eat or put on clothes that matched or go to work. I just didn't care. I felt as if I were wandering aimlessly like a zombie. People at work were noticing and asking if I was okay. I would take long bathroom breaks, disappearing for blocks of time. I was escaping to break down. I would hold it together as long as possible at my desk and then need a release. I was losing my grip. Nothing seemed to matter. I had failed yet again. God had told me to talk to Christian; I did and he chose someone else.

Even worse, Josie noticed. It was evident. I was not acting like myself. She would ask if I was okay and why I was sad. I would tell her that I was happy for her daddy but sad for me. I was as honest as I could be without getting into any details. She never knew what had happened just six months prior.

I was so confused and angry at God. How could *this* be what He had planned for my life? How could *this* be a hope and a future? I stopped reading my Bible. I stopped doing anything constructive. I was so defeated. And Satan loved it.

I would wake in the morning and he would tell me to go back to sleep. I would put my feet on the floor and the devil would be in my face telling me, "Why even try?" He mocked me. He mocked my God. He laughed at my efforts. He reminded me over and over and over how pathetic I was to think that Christian would ever want me. He reminded me of how Christian didn't want me in our marriage and what a fool I was to think that had changed.

The bad part about all of this was that I was listening. I had given up. I couldn't see how any of this would turn out good. I didn't want to be awake on the day Christian married another woman. I honestly didn't think I could live through it . . . and there was the great liar reminding me that I didn't have to. He told me the solution was obvious. And I didn't argue back. I just listened.

As a single mom, there is no good time to cry or to be pathetic. There isn't much time for anything, to be honest. You are in a constant go mode trying to make sure all of your ducks are in a row: "Are you clean? Do you have clothes for school? Did you brush your teeth? Is your bag together and ready to go? Did you charge your computer? Do you have enough lunch money? Do you have a snack for after school? Did I sign what I needed to sign? Okay, so-and-so is picking you up today. I will be there as soon after work as I can be. I love you! Have a good day."

Rush back home. Feed the dogs. Feed the cat. Turn off the lights. Turn down the air. Every penny counts. Take a quick shower. Try to find clean clothes that look decent and don't need to be ironed.

Eat something. Brush teeth. Check doors. Lock back door. Keys, keys, keys, where are my keys? Which bag did I carry yesterday? Crap! I left my purse in the car.

Throw on house shoes. Check car. There is my bag. Whew. Start up car. Let it run. Unplug toaster. Off, off, off. Everything is off.

Grab checkbook. What bills are due? Gotta pay electric and water soon.

Rushing, rushing, rushing. Hop in car. Do I have my makeup bag? Battle traffic. Throw on powder and mascara between traffic jams.

Work, work, work. Try to keep my thoughts on work. Try not to cry at work. Try to look like I have it together.

Lie and blame it on my sinuses acting up. My eyes. I need cucumber patches. Only three more hours. Almost through another day.

Who is getting Josie? Oh yeah. Work, work, work.

Finally, it's 4:30 p.m. Time to go, go, go. Try to beat traffic. Radio. Tears, tears, tears.

Traffic. Crap. Put on sunglasses so no one sees. Drive. Focus on the road. Pull it together. Tears, tears, tears. Josie can't see me like this.

Arrive. Clean up face. Get Josie. "How was your day, sweet Girlie?" Put on a smile. Keep my chin up. Be a positive mom. Turn on the tunes. Sing. Anything so I don't have to think.

Get home. Hey, puppies. Hello, kitty. Four mouths needing to be fed. All eyes on me. Dinner. TV trays. TV on. Eating. Small chats. Homework. Thirty more minutes of TV. Bedtime.

"Did you brush your teeth? Do you have clothes for tomorrow? No?" Okay, laundry. Clean kitchen. Tears, tears, tears.

"Mom, can I have some water?" "Sure, honey." Wipe tears. Check face. Deliver the water. Kiss my sweet Girl. Check the laundry. Move clothes to the dryer. Sit on my gray couch. Think. Tears, tears, tears.

God, help me sleep tonight.
God, I don't want to wake up tomorrow.
God, help me.

Alarm nagging me at 6:00 a.m. Hit snooze. Alarm nagging. Snooze. Alarm nagging. Snooze. Alarm nagging. Okay, okay!

Feet on the floor.

"Are you clean? Do you have clothes for school? Did you brush your teeth? Is your bag together and ready to go? Did you charge your computer? Do you have enough lunch money? Do you have a snack for after school? Did I sign what I needed to sign?"

Here I go again.

Chapter 30

Around the Bin

"Don't cry because it's over, smile because it happened."

—Dr. Seuss

I was a mess. In a matter of weeks, I had completely changed. I felt bruised, beaten, and defeated. My smile seemed buried. I didn't know if it would return. Friends were getting concerned. My college roommate, who was one of my best friends, decided to come be with me for the weekend of the wedding.

I couldn't believe this was happening. I really couldn't. In fact, up until the very last hour, I had a sliver of hope that Christian might change his mind and God would come through and heal my family unit. I was amazed at how deeply ingrained this hope and belief of my family was. How had I ignored it so long? Why was it so easy to push away and put off then, but so strong and so clear now? I felt chaotic, confused, and lost. Where would I go from here? *God must have a last-minute plan to save my family. He must.*

Marie came in from Dallas. She knew when she saw me it was bad. Over that weekend, she held me many times and just let me cry. She helped me go through old photos and memories and put them away for good. I wanted all of it out of sight. I needed to cleanse my home of what used to be.

We spent that Saturday going through albums of pictures from college, from a camp we had all worked at together, from my dating years with Christian, from our first years of marriage—from my pregnant pics, from photos of Josie as a newborn, from her growing, from holidays, trips, days at home, all of it. I looked at all of them one last time and was flooded with so many good memories . . . ones I had buried under resentment, anger, and hurt. It felt good to go back and see that there were smiles, laughter, and love all those years ago. It was painful, but with Marie by my side, it was doable. She made it almost enjoyable to walk down memory lane.

We shared stories of moments we remembered at college. We even laughed some. She was my angel that weekend, and I know I could not have done that well without her.

We went to a local supermarket and bought a big gold plastic tub. It was huge, but it had to be large enough to put in our old 18 x 24 family picture from when Josie was a toddler. I thought she might like to have it when she got older. All of this was for her anyway. I wanted a bin of "good memories" for her to have that would tell the story of how her mom and dad fell in love. I wanted her to know she was born in love. The big gold bin was our story for her to walk through one day.

After we had placed all of the items in the bin, I closed it with a heavy heart. I was so very sad, but yet in a way so very thankful I was able to live all of it. God had given me so many wonderful experiences. I decided to place a notecard on the outside that read, "Don't cry because it's over; smile because it happened."

I still hoped that later that evening I would hear the doorbell ring and that Christian would be there telling me he couldn't do it, that he just couldn't marry another woman. But I never heard that doorbell ring. And at some point that evening, Christian committed his life to someone else.

Chapter 31

The Final Shot in the Dark

"It's always darkest before the dawn."
—Thomas Fuller

I called Tate a week or so after Christian and I decided to let each other go. It had been almost six weeks since we had spoken. He was happy to hear my voice, but he wasn't surprised by the news. He said he had been doing well, and that he wasn't seeing anyone else.

I had hurt him, and he was confused by my emotions around Christian being with Rachel. Who could blame him? Heck, I was confused myself. I tried my best to let emotions come and process them in the now. I had learned that if I put them off, they would only return again and again until they were dealt with. So much had happened in the last six months; it almost seemed a big blur. I was numb. Although we were back to communicating frequently by phone, Tate was keeping a safe distance from me—both emotionally and physically—until one particular Thursday afternoon.

The Thursday after Marie had flown home, I decided to stay home from work. I had hit my limit of what I could take emotionally, and I wanted to shut down. I was going through the motions of everyday life, just waiting until I could get back in bed and sleep. It was the exact opposite of my normally energetic, outgoing, lively personality. I couldn't muster up the needed energy to go to work and pretend all was well. Being in sales is a tough gig to fake when you feel destroyed on the inside. I loathed my attitude, and my face had never looked so harsh. I was still mad at God for not playing according to my rules. All of this was not in the plan, not *my plan*, anyway. I hadn't talked to God in many, many days. Someone else was filling my head with chatter. And it scared me how easy it was to listen to Satan and believe the lies he was feeding me.

After getting Josie to school that morning, I came home and crawled back in bed. I slept until my head hurt. When I woke up, I noticed Tate had called me a couple of times, and his texts showed he was worried that I had not responded. The latest text from him read, "Scarlett, are you okay? Please let me know you are all right." It was all I could do to cradle the cell phone in my hands. For the first time ever, I typed the following: "I am not good" and placed it on my nightstand.

My phone rang immediately. It was Tate. I didn't answer. It rang again. I didn't answer.

I slowly rolled out of bed and shuffled the few feet to my dresser where I kept a small gun, a .22-caliber Ruger that Tate had given me a couple of years ago. I wasn't very familiar with guns and had only shot this particular one twice. It felt cold and heavy as I lifted it out of my lingerie drawer.

I just wanted to hold it. I just wanted to look at it and feel it in my hand. It felt powerful, but I felt everything but that.

My phone rang again. I didn't answer. I was staring at the small Ruger. A hot tear fell from my face as I listened to the thoughts flooding my mind. I felt as if I had a dozen demons circled around me—some climbing on me—all chattering thoughts of condemnation and hatred at me at all at once. My head was spinning. I wanted to hold the cold metal to my head. I wanted silence.

My pursuer became my protector.

Another tear fell. Then another. I wanted to sleep, to quiet my mind and make it all stop. I was so broken in that moment, and I felt so sorry for myself. I kept thinking, *It would be better this way.* And my mind drifted to thoughts that were not of God and not my own. It was obvious Satan was whispering his plan for my demise into my ear, but I was too tired to fend him off. It was easier to listen to him in the moment, and everything he whispered made sense to me. The thought came again as I looked down at the gun: *Maybe it would be better this way . . .*

The phone rang again, and I snapped out of my daze. I placed the gun on my bed close to my pillow, picked up the phone, and answered without saying a word.

"Scarlett! Hello? Are you there? Hello? Scarlett? Are you there? Are you okay?"

"I'm not too good," I faintly whispered through my tears. I could hardly breathe as I sat down on the bed.

"I'm coming over. I'm coming right now!" Tate spat the words out with a strong sense of urgency.

"No. No. I don't want you here," I said, more alert. I stood up, frantically pacing about, noticing my messy house. I didn't want anyone to see me this way, let alone Tate.

"Scarlett, something is wrong. I feel it. I am coming over and that is that. Stay right there. Don't do anything, okay? Just stay right there. Promise me, Scarlett. Promise me!"

I sat down on the couch, crying. I let the phone fall to the floor without ending the call. I wanted to get up, go to my room, pick up that .22, and sleep forever. I just wanted to stop hurting. I wanted rest. I wanted to stop thinking. I had never felt so exhausted in my life.

Through the blur of tears I saw Josie's picture on the wall. My Josie. My sweet Josie Rose. And I started to bawl like a baby. What was wrong with me? What would Josie do without me? What would she think if I gave up? How would this change her life? She was such a happy, sweet, carefree girl. She was so lovely. I always taught her to never give up, and here I was, wanting to quit. What legacy would that leave for her? The chatter began again . . . *God, you're such a pathetic loser . . . Just end it already . . .*

The doorbell rang, followed by frantic beating on the door. "Scarlett! Scarlett, it's me! Open the door!"

I opened the door, my face a mess, my nose running, tears smeared all over my cheeks. Tate was so concerned. I had never seen his face so worried. He opened the screen door and embraced me, kissing the top of my head and holding me tight.

And I cried. I cried so hard I couldn't catch my breath.

"It's okay, Scarlett. It's okay. Everything is going to be okay."

We embraced for what seemed like an eternity because it was difficult for me to stand. He walked me to the couch, sat me down, and asked if he could get me anything. I shook my head and stared blankly. He walked away from the couch and disappeared out of my line of vision. I sat there in a fog.

Then from my bedroom, he yelled, "What is this? What is this, Scarlett!? What are you doing?" He had found the .22 on my bed. He came around the corner with my gun in his hand, but I couldn't look at it. I was ashamed.

"I don't know. I don't know. I . . . I just wanted to hold it, Tate. I just . . . I just wanted to have it there. I just wanted it there. I don't know, Tate. Don't be mad. I wasn't . . . I wasn't going to . . . I wouldn't." He rushed over and sat by me. My words were as emotionless as my eyes. There was simply no life left within me.

He was angry. "This is *stupid*, Scarlett! Do you hear me? This is stupid!"

"I wasn't going to, Tate. I was just looking at it. I just wanted it close. I just—"

"Scarlett, you don't even need this out! Do you understand? This is not good. What would Josie do? What would she do, Scarlett? I'm taking this. I'm putting it in my car, and I am taking it away from here. I am also staying tonight. Got it? I am staying, and I will be with you. Everything is going to be okay. I'm not leaving you. Do you understand?"

After a long pause, I looked at him and said, "Why are you here, Tate? Why? I am a mess. I messed it all up. I messed up my family. It's gone forever. I messed it up."

"Scarlett, I love you. Can't you believe that? Why can't you just believe it? I know. I know it hurts. I know you messed up. I messed up. We messed up. Christian messed up. Vicky messed up. We all made a mess of things. But it's going to be okay. I love you. I am here for you. That's just how it is. You were always there for me. When I lost everything and didn't have a penny to my name, you were there for me. Even when you were honest about your inkling you were there for me. That was our pact. You honored that. I love that about you.

"You are a strong woman, Scarlett. You just don't realize how strong you are. Change is hard sometimes, but you will be okay. That's just the type of woman you are. You fall and you get up. You just have to get up one more time than you fall." He grinned his gentle grin, determined he could will me into believing there was hope. Tate always knew how to talk to me. He always knew exactly what to say.

And he was right. Everything was going to be okay.

It's funny how God works. Just when you think you can't take anymore, just when you are about to give up, He sends you a lifeline.

I learned a lot in the three weeks that lead up to the devil's final shot at wiping me off the grid. I learned to never stop talking to God, no matter how hurt or how mad or how disappointed I am. None of my emotions or circumstances are a surprise to God. He knows and He understands my feelings and my shortcomings. And He loves me anyway.

Tate came to my rescue that day, and he did stay with me that night. He held me all night and was there to protect me from myself. Tate, who had been my pursuer, became my protector. Funny how God works.

Chapter 32

The Little Wooden Maiden in a Purple Dress

"Just because the past didn't turn out like you wanted it to, doesn't mean your future can't be better than you've ever imagined."
—Anonymous

It was now nearly six weeks after the wedding, and I had calmed down. My internal control-freak had finally surrendered. Obviously, God had other plans in mind for my life, and I just needed to trust Him. I was quiet and humbled and at peace. It was almost like I had been at war, internally fighting for the redemption I wanted and what I believed could be the only answer to the mess I made. I finally relinquished my delusional control. Life sure was a lot easier now that I wasn't trying to control it.

I was no longer responsible for Christian. I no longer had to worry about him or feel guilty that he was missing out on Josie. He had made his choice, and I was completely free. In His infinite wisdom, I believe God knew I needed to give Christian the chance he felt he never got. That way I would truly feel like I did everything I could do to save my family, and I could have the peace I needed to move on with my life. I also believe it was healing for Christian to say no to me. And maybe that was just what he needed to move on with his life. God knew Christian and me better than we knew ourselves. The confusion of what God had asked me to do was all making sense now.

Josie still had not breathed a word about the wedding. I didn't know whether to think it was odd or normal. After all, I had never been through this, and neither had she. When my mother remarried, I was about Josie's age and I was at the ceremony. I recall it was an odd feeling watching my mom get married. I felt that if Josie wanted to talk about the wedding, she would, so I didn't press her for details. I didn't ask, and she didn't say, and life carried on as normal.

One afternoon about a month and a half after her father's wedding day, I was putting away coats in our living room closet. It was customary for me to check pockets before hanging up the garments. Josie was in TV land, zoned out on cartoons. It always made me smile, knowing she got that trait honestly from Christian Robert.

As I picked up Josie's vintage fur coat to hang, I admired it for a bit, remembering the deal I had gotten it for at a sidewalk sale in a small country town nearby. I put my hand in the right side pocket and felt something odd and bumpy. I held it for a moment in my hand, almost playing a game with myself to see if I could figure out what the object was before laying eyes on it. But I had no clue. It was smooth, but had many curves and felt like a figurine of some sort.

I pulled the object out and was totally perplexed. I had never seen this item before. It was a little wooden maiden in a purple dress. I studied the wooden girl from top to bottom. She was hand-painted with intricate details. Red hair pulled into a bun with a flower-type headband and a deep purple dress with little black shoes. It looked like a little wooden figurine of Josie. Under a foot was a small mark that read, "C & R" with a date below. Then it hit me, this must be from the wedding. *It was Josie.*

I looked up almost instinctively, feeling eyes on me. Josie was staring at me, her eyes huge. She sat still as a statue waiting for my response. I asked, "Josie, is this from Daddy's wedding?"

She nodded yes, hardly breathing, still fearful of what was to come. "Yes, ma'am. It was on the cake," she said in a low, hesitant voice.

I smiled gently and walked over to the couch where she was sitting. I reached out my hand slowly to touch her sweet, soft face. I placed my fingertips under her chin and lovingly lifted her face to look toward mine.

"It's okay, Josie. It's okay. I'm happy for your daddy. I want Daddy to be happy. I want you to know it's okay for you to be happy for Daddy and for Rachel. It's okay, sweetie. Now, would you like me to put this little doll in your room? Maybe on your dresser beside the picture of you and Daddy when you were a baby?"

Josie looked at me with a big smile, so relieved and so peaceful. She said, "That would be great. Thanks, Momma." I could feel a huge weight lifting off of my Girlie.

I walked toward her room with the little wooden maiden in the purple dress resting in my palm, knowing in my spirit that God had healed even the darkest corners of my heart. He had even cleaned out all of the forgotten cob-webbed corners lurking in the shadows. I was truly free. Free indeed.

Chapter 33

He Knew

"When you are in a relationship with someone who does not meet your needs—it brings out the worst in you."

—Anonymous

Who knew the crazy counselor would be so right? When she first mentioned a failed marriage, I automatically labeled her as off her rocker and slightly coldhearted, when that wasn't true at all. She was speaking with the wisdom of more than twenty years of experience in marital counseling. She was dead-on. She hit the nail on the head, and at the time, I was too spiritually immature to accept her words of truth.

So I will save you a trip to your local counselor and possibly several hundred dollars. Here is the short of it. Make sure you are sitting for this one: Sometimes good, God-fearing, kindhearted, wonderful Christian people have failed marriages. It does *not* mean that those two people don't love each other, and it doesn't mean that they didn't love each other with their whole heart. It simply means those two people, as hard as they tried, did not meet each other's needs.

It takes more than love. It takes want-to and work. It takes two people willing to do the hard work together, willing to grow together, willing to talk, willing to listen, willing to compromise, willing to change, willing to forgive, and willing to give.

Christian and I just couldn't get our timing together. When I was willing to work, he wasn't. When he was willing to work, I wasn't. And we danced that dance until we were both too tired, too mad, too resentful, too selfish, too proud, and too brokenhearted to try anymore. It is one of the hardest lessons I have had to learn so far in life.

I was wrong. I was selfish. I had a part in my failed marriage. I failed. Who knew that our beautiful love story that had started so perfectly would end so tragically, so ugly?

He knew.

When I find myself questioning my journey, reminiscing over times past, or when I just can't make sense of it all, I remind myself that God knew. He knew all along where Christian and I would end up. He knew about Josie. He knew we would make a mess of our marriage, but that we would be the perfect parental team for our beautiful daughter. Perhaps He gave us Josie Rose so we wouldn't give up on each other. So we would be forced to communicate and work through things. He knew we would find healing in our relationship, but He knew it would look so very different from anything we could have imagined.

Isn't that what God does? He takes our messes that Satan intends for evil and molds them into beautiful stories of healing. He gives us beauty for our ashes. And beyond that, He knew I would be willing to write His story. He knew I would be willing to share. He knew that you might need these very words you are reading, so He called me to write this book.

He knew you needed hope. He knew you needed healing. He knew this story would touch your hurts and move you to become a better you. He knew that in sharing His story, it would also bring me *complete* healing. He knew that in my writing and sharing and speaking, in those things, helping you brings healing to us both. Simply amazing. It's His amazing grace.

It is now time for me to completely lay this story at His feet. It is His. It is time for me to move on to the next chapter of my life. It is time to *begin*.

Will you be bold and begin with me? It's guaranteed to be a wild ride! You just never know where God will take you if you let Him lead. Be brave. You are strong enough to close the last chapter and step out in faith to begin the next.

Friends, this isn't the end of my story or yours. It's just the beginning.

"He will give a crown of beauty for ashes"
– **Isaiah 61:3** (NLT)

Chapter 34

No Turning Back

"The course of true love never did run smooth."
—William Shakespeare

Josie Rose is eleven and a half.

At work one day I was entering some information I wanted to put into a Word document. Suddenly I noticed an unfamiliar file saved in my personal folder that I hadn't seen before. I saw Josie's name in the title and clicked on the document to figure out what it was and where it had come from.

As I read the words, tears of joy filled my eyes. My heart swelled with gladness, freedom, and a pride only a parent can know. These are the words I read:

> *I'm so proud of you, Mom. You have accomplished so much in your life. You are about to enter a new life. No turning back. ☺ You will be so pretty walking down the aisle! —Josie*

It had been a little over a year since Josie and I discussed the little wooden maiden in the purple dress. I had set her free that day emotionally. Free to enjoy her father and her new bonus mom. Now Josie was setting me free. *My daughter is proud of me.*

Josie knew my truth; I had confessed it all to her shortly after her eleventh birthday. She had forgiven me. She had watched me accept God's gift of grace and embrace His peaceful Spirit. Now she was giving me her blessing and her grace.

Those words were the most beautiful words I had ever read. In that moment, I knew I had broken the legacy of failed relationships in my family. I knew deep in my soul that Josie would not have the same struggles as I had. She wouldn't be codependent, and she wouldn't have trust issues with men. She was whole. I was whole. I loved *me* again, and I was ready to love again. Truly, deeply, unconditionally.

In just two short weeks, I was to marry Tate. God had turned my mourning into dancing. He knew all along the deepest desires of my heart.

My new chapter had begun.

Chapter 35

Leap Day

"You can't start the next chapter of your life if you keep reading the last chapter over and over."

—Anonymous

I heard the music echoing across the beach. "No Turning Back" by King and Country played loudly for all on Naples's south shore to hear. The weather was perfect, not a cloud in the sky. The sun was half an hour from setting over the ocean's gentle waves, and the sky glowed a magnificent reddish-orange, as if painted by God Himself. This was the moment I thought I would never live to see. The day I would commit my life to another man, other than Christian Robert. It was as if time was standing still.

A song I had heard a hundred times over seemed to last forever as my feet sank in the sand with each step toward Tate. I could see the bamboo arch in the distance with its draped burlap softly swaying in the breeze.

Our six dearest friends, including Jen and Marie, waited on either side of the arch, their faces glowing and their eyes glazed with tears. They knew it had been such a long road to healing for both of us, and each of them had been by our sides through it all. Eight long years of ups and downs, mountains and valleys, break-ups and reuniting, so many in-depth discussions analyzing life and love and sin and redemption. So many nights weeping over our choices, and all that those decisions had cost. So many questions. The most important one being—could God *really* bless this relationship?

Tate and I had weathered the gamut of life together over the last decade. We had both had everything before. We had healthy families, nice homes, solid jobs, a church support system, and good reputations in our communities. Ultimately, we both lost all of that together. We had both been the one who caused so much destruction in each other's lives. Yet here we were, ready to begin trying to build all of that back with one another.

There was so much irony in our union. *But God.* In His own mysterious but perfect way, God allowed us to see how good He was in forgiving us both. Not just redeeming, but blessing us both in tremendous ways— Tate in his business, and I in my newly founded ministry. And because of Christ's unconditional love, I was able to forgive Tate for all the hurt and dysfunction he had brought to my life. And vice versa. We chose each other because we were the only two people on the planet who understood the depth of sorrow we had each endured, and knew just how hard we had both worked to get out of that despair to where we were now.

I had never seen a man so willing to work on himself. So willing to take ownership of his actions, accept his failures, and take the consequences like a champ. Both of us worked incredibly hard on ourselves to understand where our dysfunction came from. We had spent years of individual and couple's counseling, dissecting our family dynamics, learning to understand our inner-child, and attaining tools to process and release the pain of where we had been, in order to never again become the individuals we were over a decade ago.

We never said, "Why me?" We knew *why us*. We knew all the loss was our own doing. And here we were, still willing to accept each other, baggage and all.

As I got closer to Tate, I saw his tears falling onto his white linen shirt. It was such a serene moment. We both we so proud of who the other had become, and it shined through our gentle grins to each other. The warm sea-salt air drifted across my face as I took the last step and reached my hands toward his. We stood face-to-face holding hands, as the minister led the simple, but perfect ceremony.

We had both crafted our vows to one another. I had notes and Tate spoke from his heart. Then sand from two jars flowed into one, representing our two lives enmeshing together. Our lips touched for the first time as husband and wife, indicating that we had done the deed. Tate's expression was so humble and so proud at the same time.

Moments later, our small wedding party danced on the beach to Wilson Phillips' classic tune "Hold On," as pictures were taken. I laughed and frolicked like I never thought possible, after all I had been through.

Not only was it special because it was our wedding day; it was also Leap Day, February 29—a day created to straighten out the mess of the calendar. We chose it for that exact purpose. Now, it was our day—the day we set things straight with our own mess.

There really was no turning back, just like the song, and we were eager to be in our new chapter of life together. It was a glorious time, and we danced until the sunset over the water.

"You turned my mourning into dancing."
—Psalm 30:11

Chapter 36

Hot Mess to Hot Bless

"You can't out-sin God."
—Michelle Moore

Three weeks after I became Mrs. Tate Rogers...

I sat beside Josie on the couch as she watched TV. There wasn't much else to do in the two-bedroom apartment we were all currently crammed in. As I looked around, I laughed out loud.

"What, Momma? What's so funny?"

"Well, Girlie, this isn't exactly the lake house Tate and I promised you. It looks more like a hoarder's apartment." I laughed out loud again, this time even louder. She began to giggle too.

"The house should be ready soon, Momma. We are almost there!"

"I know, Sweetie. It's just hilarious."

We were building our dream home. It was so very exciting! Tate had purchased a piece of property that bordered the lake about four years back. He had always told me he would build me a lake house. Of course, me being so skeptical of marriage and the "dream life," I would always shake my head, roll my eyes, and blow him off. However, he was definitely proving me wrong.

We were now only weeks away from our new home being complete! We had sold my little three-bedroom, two-bath house and were now all residing in Tate's two-bedroom, two-bath apartment. Three people, two elderly dogs, and a cat—all trying to function among piles of furniture, and walls upon walls of plastic totes.

We had somehow managed to fit all of my household items and all of Tate's household items into his 1,100-square-foot apartment and the detached garage he was also leasing. Needless to say, there was not much space to move about.

Shiloh, my fourteen-year-old lab-corgi mix with dementia, moseyed in front of us. "Poor Shiloh. She has no idea where she is," I said out loud.

"Wonder how she will do in the new house, Momma?" Josie enquired.

"I'm not sure, Girlie. She is very confused. Bless her."

Every day for the past year, Shiloh would slowly pace the parameter of our old home. If something was in her way, she would go over it, never around it. If she couldn't go over it, she would just stand there until someone moved whatever it was in her way. Sometimes, we would find her stuck in a corner just standing there, staring straight ahead, not even trying to get out. It was pitiful, but now she was on medicine that was helping her nerves, thanks to Rachel.

I never dreamed Josie's bonus mom would be such a help to my pups and I, but she was. In fact, I would say she was one of the best veterinarians I had ever encountered, and I would often jest with Christian Robert that he chose well.

Shiloh still had a healthy body, so we let her continue her rounds. With all the change, I could not bear to say goodbye to my Shiloh-girl just yet. She and her brother Colby had truly been my constants through all of the ups and downs of the past fourteen years. They were like my children, and even Josie called them Sissy and Bubba. They were the only siblings she had known.

It was amazing what wonderful pets they both were. Together they had cost Christian and I a total of $70 for the adoption at a local humane shelter. At only six weeks old, the two pups were so close that we could not think of splitting them up. So we decided to adopt them both. It was one of the best decisions we had made in our nearly ten married years. Colby and Shiloh were companions to us both, and brought unconditional love and pure joy through so many years of hardship. If there were ever such a thing as a four-legged angel, I believe God had blessed us with two.

Three more weeks had passed and we managed to not kill one another, or any of the animals, while living in the apartment. Finally our dream home on the lake was complete! It was the most beautiful home I had ever seen, and I could not believe it was going to be ours! In all my years, I never dreamed I would live in a big home, much less a big home on the lake.

I had always loved water growing up. I was a fish in the water as a child, and Tate and I both were lifeguards in our teen years. I also loved creeks. As a little girl, I could remember dreaming of owning a home one day with a creek in the back yard. This home had a creek and a lake, with almost two acres of beautiful rolling woods surrounding us. It was a dream come true.

As we turned the key to our new home for the first time, Tate declared, "God is so good!" We stepped inside to a pristine open floor plan with shiny hardwood floors, earth-toned stone columns, windows wherever your eyes landed, wood beams on the high ceiling, and the most magnificent view I had ever seen! It was more than we could have ever imagined or dreamed for ourselves. All three of us teared up and stood huddled in a hug with the biggest grins on our faces. God was giving us double for our trouble. Our pastor had drilled this theory into our heads, but walking in His blessing and favor was completely overwhelming in the moment.

Tate and I knew we did not deserve this house. We knew what we actually deserved had happened over two thousand years ago on the cross. But Jesus had paid the price for our debt owed, and His grace was sufficient.

All those times the devil had told me that God would never bless me after what I had done was being proved wrong at every turn. What a liar! And how arrogant of me to think that I could out-sin God's grace. Who did I think I was?! So Jesus's blood could atone everyone's sin in the entire world, but not my adultery?

I was seeing so clearly now. God *can* bless a mess! Even when you cause the *mess*. He can take a hot mess and turn it into a hot bless.

Don't you see? We can never out-sin God. It just isn't possible! Jesus took on all the sins of the entire world at once. He knew exactly what sin He was covering for me and for you and for everyone else, when He shed His precious blood for us.

I had a new found peace. I now understood that God was never surprised. He knew all along . . . and He still loved me. He still sent His son to die for me. If He was willing to do that, despite my sin, I was now beginning to see there was *nothing* He could not do. There was no blessing He wanted to keep from me.

I was the one who had waited so long to accept His gift. I was the one who had taken my own sweet time surrendering to Him. And now that I had, I was walking in His amazing grace.

"My cup overflows."
—Psalm 23:5

Chapter 37

Forever Sleep

"Greater love has no one than this:
to lay down one's life for one's friends."
—John 15:13 (NIV)

It was fall of our first married year. Josie Rose is twelve.
Seven months after moving into our new home, I sat in my parked car, outside of my chiropractor's office, head on the steering wheel, bawling like a baby. Mascara was smeared all over my tear-soaked face. And the noises coming out of me were ones that I had not heard since the first weekend of "child swap" when I was left alone without my heart, my sweet Josie Rose. Except this time, I wasn't crying because I was sad. I was crying because I was overjoyed.

Who does this? Who sits in their car crying over how wonderful the new wife of their ex-husband is? Even typing the very words seems absurd. Nevertheless, that's exactly what I was doing.

I was awe-struck. I was enamored. I was humbled. I was thankful. This woman had shown me love. Me—the first wife of her first husband. The one who broke him in. The one who won't go away. The mother of her husband's first child. Me. The last person on earth who should be showing emotion over how truly lovely my daughter's bonus mom is. But I was. And I gave in to it. I let it all flow out of me like a gushing ink pen. Messy. Ugly. And sure to leave marks.

A few days earlier, on Saturday afternoon, Rachel had driven over an hour to visit our new home out in the country. She had already put in a half day's work at her vet clinic, and I am sure she would have much rather spent the rest of the day hiking with Christian Robert or gone home for a bite to eat and a nap. But instead, she spent her Saturday afternoon providing end-of-life care for my almost fifteen-year-old furry baby girl, Shiloh. The perfect blend of yellow lab and corgi, thoughts of how Shiloh's mom and dad must have made that arrangement work always made me giggle.

So much change had occurred in my life since bringing Shiloh and Colby home, from becoming a new mom and bringing Josie home, and slowly introducing our current "children" to the new bundle of joy. To me adjusting to becoming a stay-at-home-mom, and days crying with them both at my side on the kitchen floor, wondering if I was any good at this *mom thing*. To me throwing fits when I was angry because Josie wouldn't nap, to when I was missing my identity as a professional, to when I was sad because I felt so alone, to when I started to lose myself and fell into a relationship with another man . . . Shiloh and Colby were always there. Always loving me the same. Always so excited to see me.

When I lost my job, my marriage, my reputation, my church family, my extended family, and many friends because of my affair . . . Shiloh and Colby were there. All through my journey, the two beings on this planet who never saw me any differently and loved me just as I was, right where I was, were my precious puppies. And on this day, I would have to say goodbye to one of them.

Over the last few months, Shiloh had become so frail, she was truly like a skeleton of the dog she once was. She had battled dementia for the past two years. Her eyes were glazed over, and I often wondered if she was even there. But on her good days, she would stop circling the outskirts of the living room and kitchen to stop at my feet for some loving rubs. I would bend down to her to tell her what a good girl she was, what a pretty girl she was. She would look deep in my eyes, as if she knew me and knew I was a safe person, but couldn't quite place why or who I was. I would kiss her forehead as many times as she would allow before she took off again to walk her rounds. I can still hear her dragging her right paw, nails lightly scraping the wood floors, as she paced around. It had become a comforting sound.

I chuckled to myself, remembering the time I tried to attach my FitBit to her leg to earn some no-effort steps. Unfortunately, it didn't register her steps.

But on this day, Rachel, lovely Rachel, came to my home so Shiloh could fall into her forever sleep in the comforts of her safe haven. Shiloh had become a nervous wreck if I tried to carry her anywhere in the car. Her teeth would audibly chatter with nervousness. It was pitiful. And I just didn't want to put her through that again.

Rachel gave me time with her before injecting the sedative. She walked me through each step and told me to take my time. I was able to hold Shiloh in my arms on her favorite napping spot on our living room rug. It was about as perfect and peaceful as a goodbye could be. So comfortable for me and for my sweet four-legged girl. Then it happened—Shiloh drifted away from me slowly, gently, and pain-free. I sobbed as I held her limp body, and Rachel stepped outside with Christian and Josie Rose to give me time alone. Tate held me as I held Shiloh. It was a hard but beautiful moment.

Over the next two days, I stayed in bed, unable to stop crying. I physically ached over the loss, just like I had lost a child. I felt so silly for grieving so deeply over an animal, but a piece of my heart died that day and my world would not be the same.

I had cared for elderly-Shiloh for so long that I almost didn't know what to do with myself after she was gone. My daily routine revolved around her—medicine, feeding, carrying her outside for potty breaks, constant supervision of her pacing, naptime, and more medicine after dinner. Most days I hand fed her each morsel of food because she had forgotten how to eat. It truly was like caring for an elderly family member with memory loss.

On the third day, I'd finally left the house to go to a chiropractic appointment and was reflecting on all that had transpired, when I felt moved in my heart to call Rachel and personally thank her for all she had done to help care for Shiloh. I called the vet clinic and through my tears, I expressed how grateful I was for her. How impressed I was with her going out of her way for my puppies and me. How it meant the world to me how she treated Shiloh as her own. How it meant so much to me that she treats my daughter as her own.

And then it happened . . . I began to talk about Christian Robert with her. Like a blubbering fool caught up in my emotion over my deceased dog, I somehow started explaining how I never could *reach* my ex-husband and how I had prayed for God to send a woman he would listen to. A woman he would respect who could help bring him back, help him thrive, and help him find his smile again. I told her what an answered prayer she had been, and that I could see how happy Christian was again, and how truly happy I was for them. And how it meant so much to me that Josie had her dad back.

I was met with a gracious "You're welcome," followed by a lot of silence. Who could blame her? Poor soul. What do you say when the ex-wife is going on and on about how blessed she is to have you in her ex-husband's and daughter's life? You couldn't make this stuff up. She was probably waiting to see if she was on an episode of *Punked*. Bless.

I finally shut up and hung up the phone, and there I sat in the parking lot with a tear-stained face and a grateful heart. Josie Rose was one blessed child. She would not know it for many years, but the peaceful, generous, respectful relationship that her father, myself, and her stepmother all shared was such a gift to her.

My daughter walks in emotional freedom. Freedom to enjoy both families and both homes with no guilt or shame. She does not have to be in the middle of communication dysfunction, due to divorce. She does not know the pain of resentment and bitterness brewing in her parents.

Again, I was seeing God's masterpiece come together. Every desire of my heart seemed to be unfolding before me. I was in awe. God had done it again. He took what the devil intended for harm, and used it to bless Josie. He took our divorce and beautifully crafted two supportive families for my daughter, instead of just one. Josie had the most outstanding support system of anyone I had ever known. More and more, I was beginning to trust God's plan over my own.

Chapter 38

Then There Were Four

"The Joy of the Lord is my strength."
— Nehemiah 8:10

Josie will be a teenager soon.

I had just dropped Josie off with her father for the weekend. It was a successful swap, and all bags were safely delivered into Christian's vehicle. No new conversations were tackled, and I wished them both a great weekend. I hugged and kissed Josie, said my good-byes, and Tate and I drove away.

We decided to go eat dinner after we met up with Christian. I reached for Tate's hand and he reached for mine, almost instinctively meeting in the middle over the gearshift. We sat in silence holding hands, appreciating the peace of the moment. We were so grateful that we all got along. It was truly a miracle after all we had endured.

Josie was always excited to see her dad. They had a lot of fun together. I was thankful that Christian was her father. He was a good one, and he had continued to prove that, even after two years of marriage to another woman.

A lot of men change after re-marriage. They leave one family and cling to the new one as if changing people will help them escape their guilt and regret of past decisions made. I was so grateful Christian had not taken that path. Instead, he remained the rock Josie needed him to be. I recognized that in him and often let him know how much I appreciated what a good father he was. I believe being appreciative in a co-parenting relationship is key.

He always paid child support on time. He always showed up for Josie and attended her games and band recitals. He encouraged her to have social time and did not put his selfish desires in the way of their weekends. He called her almost every day to check-in, talk to her about her day, check on school assignments, and tell her he loved her. Christian normally knew more than I did about her schoolwork and was a constant encouragement to her academically. Their solid father-daughter relationship showed through in her self-confidence and self-esteem as a now teenage girl.

Raising a well-balanced, emotionally healthy child *is* possible within divorced families. The devil will lie to you and say it isn't possible, but Josie Rose was living proof that with God, forgiveness, respect, and appreciation of both parents one to the other, it was absolutely possible.

On the way to the restaurant, I heard the muffled ding of a text message. I dug for my phone in my purse and saw it was a message from Christian. I thought that was curious because we had just parted ways not even five minutes prior. Maybe they had forgotten something? I opened the message and began to read it: "I just wanted you to know that Rachel is expecting. We plan to tell Josie this weekend."

I was completely taken aback and couldn't catch my breath. The wind was knocked out of me for only the second time in my life. The first was when I was an eleven-year-old girl in a beginner karate class and I got kicked straight in the gut by an upper-belt. This feeling was similar, like a punt right to the gut. Tears immediately began to flood my eyes and stream down my face uncontrollably. Everything seemed to be spinning. I began gasping for air.

"Baby! Are you okay? What is it? What's the matter?!" Tate burst out.

I was hyperventilating. The pain in my chest was distantly familiar. I needed air. Unable to speak, grabbing my chest and my throat, I motioned for Tate to pull over. He jerked the car into the first parking lot available, a Waffle House. I threw off my seatbelt and as soon as the car came to somewhat of a halt, I slung open the door and jumped out. I ran to the nearest grassy area and collapsed on my knees, gasping for air. Breath finally filled my lungs, and I let out a wail of a mother who had just lost her child. The pain of that moment was indescribable.

Tate rushed to my side, holding me and rocking with me, asking over and over again. "What is it? What is the matter, baby!?"

I couldn't look at him. I just couldn't.

I continued to wail and moan. In that moment, all I felt was the loss of the baby that should have been mine. The baby the devil stole from me. The sibling that should be in my house with Josie and my family.

A tidal wave of anger and regret and shame and terror and misunderstanding flooded back to me, as if I had never healed from all that occurred a decade ago. A piece of my soul felt like it was dying all over again right, there on the side lawn of the Waffle House.

Tate attempted to peel me up off the ground, but I wouldn't have it. I didn't want him touching me. I didn't want anyone touching me. No one knew how this felt.

"Scarlett, please. You're scaring me," Tate pleaded.

I pushed him away, shaking my head, still not able to look at him. I kneeled there sobbing for at least five more minutes, but it felt like thirty. I stayed until I had no more tears or energy to give, until I felt like a zombie with glassed over eyes.

After the light comes the fight.

I began to unearth myself and reluctantly trudged back to our car where a very concerned Tate was patiently waiting. He still had no idea what I had read. I opened the car door, placed one foot onto the floorboard, and slinked down into the bucket seat.

He asked me one more time what had happened. I couldn't say the words without losing it again, so I handed him my phone for him to see the message for himself.

"Oh, Scarlett. I'm so sorry. It's going to be okay." He said softly and cautiously.

Tate knew I wanted more kids. It was something I made clear before we married. I would joke with him often about having a baby, but he was not interested. In our conversations about more children, Tate would say *maybe* . . . but I knew his answer was more to please me, and not because he really wanted another child. Tate was older than me and had three of his own, plus one bonus kiddo in Josie. He felt like his season for kids had passed, and he knew this would be challenging for me to accept.

In truth, at this point, I had *not* accepted this. I was still very hopeful for a baby and prayed often for one. And now I felt as if Christian and Rachel were getting the very thing *I had been praying for.*

I sat staring out the car window, much like the night I told Christian Robert the truth about my affair. I thought to myself, *I've been here before.* And I knew, as I knew back then, from this day forward, life was never going to be the same.

How ironic. This time, Christian was the bearer of the news. *How long must I feel the pain of those terrible choices from over twelve years ago?* Life was connected. My choices way back then led to this very moment, some twelve-plus years later. I knew I had opened the door to this loss by choosing to step outside of my marriage. I knew that the devil loved this moment. I knew light had been in my life. I knew my ministry was making a difference. The devil knew too, and he wanted to knock me back. After the light, comes the fight.

A new battle had just begun. Another round of head-to-head battles with regret, bitterness, guilt, shame, and anger. At the moment, I had no idea if I even had a chance in this mental battle. It felt like too much.

Chapter 39

Greener Grass Grows Twice as Fast

"Bless your ex. Bless your kids."
—**Scarlett Rose**

Winter was upon us.

Nothing can prepare you for watching your ex build a family with someone else. The devil doesn't show you that when he's tempting you with a *season of fun*. He shows you the greener grass but doesn't show you that you still have to mow it. He doesn't show you how much harder you'll have to work to keep up that greener grass because it grows twice as fast, and the mower needs constant maintenance. He doesn't show you the choppy, rut-filled land that lies underneath that greener grass.

I was quickly learning that working on your second blended family was twice as much work. I wanted to shout from the mountaintops, "Save your first family! Do whatever it takes, people!"

Instead of working twice as hard on your second family, and splitting the time with your children, rotating holidays and birthdays, why not work half as hard on your first family and still be together? My hindsight was twenty-twenty. It was something Tate and I talked about often.

We both agreed as wonderful as our life was now and as blessed as we were, if we could go back, we would not make those same selfish choices. If we knew then what we had discovered in the now, we would stay and work on our first families. However, that was not possible. We also knew our journey of terrible choices and loss had created the wise people we were today. We had been refined by the Refiner's fire.

I prayed daily for my ex-husband and his wife. As a child of divorce myself, I knew the best path to ensure Josie was secure, free, and happy in her own skin, was to wish blessings and favor on her father. How can a child thrive in a hostile, awkward, emotionally strained environment? They cannot. How can they feel free to enjoy both homes if there is no peace between those homes? They cannot.

As divorced parents, Christian and I decided long ago that it was not about us anymore. We had both had our chances, and we had both blown it. It takes two to make a marriage, and it takes two to break a marriage. Our time had passed. We failed, and we both owned it. Now, it was about Josie Rose. How can we ensure she wins?

The answer was by both being for her, and both being for each other. We needed to be on the same team, working together, to move our daughter down the field of life, cheering her on from the same side. It was clear—the best way to bless Josie was to bless Christian. I knew it in my soul like I knew the sky was blue.

Every day I prayed that Christian would receive all the desires of his heart, that he would be joy-filled, prospered, protected, and that God would create in him the father Josie needed him to be, in order for her to become the young warrior of God He needed her to be for His kingdom. Every day that I prayed for Christian, I had peace and a virtuous attitude toward him and Rachel in that day.

Now that the desires for his heart were coming to pass, I was faced with a decision. Bitter or better? Resentful or joyful? If I truly wanted goodness and blessings and favor for Christian, how could I make this blessing all about me? I couldn't. And if I let this grief take me out, how could Josie be free to enjoy her sister or brother? She couldn't.

This was obviously not about me. So I decided to take three days to process my pain. I cried and wailed and yelled at God with everything in me for those seventy-two hours. I cursed at Him. I demanded why this, after all I had done obeying His lead in my ministry. It was ugly. But it was gut-wrenching honest. And that was what my relationship with my Heavenly Father had become. I walked and talked with Him daily. He had become my best friend. And I had to be honest with Him that He had peeved me off.

On the third day of processing, I went outside on our upper balcony, which overlooked our wooded acreage, and I could see the lake peeking through the bare limbs of winter. It was freezing outside, but I didn't care. I needed to be hit with the chilly, fresh air.

I was emotionally exhausted. I had screamed my last scream. I had no more tears in my tank. I sat down Indian style on the decorative outdoor rug on our deck. Above me was an A-line wood beam covering with a ceiling fan. It was whirling from the chilly winter gusts that were caressing my bare face. I hadn't put makeup on in three days, and I didn't care. I felt naked before God physically, emotionally, mentally, and was now spiritually. I sat surrendered in silence, listening for something. Anything. I needed to hear from God. I needed His wisdom.

I cried out gently from my spirit. "Why God? Why this?" I sat still, waiting.

He spoke. "You wanted a sibling for Josie."

I heard it clearly in my spirit and exhaled a sigh of defeat. God was right. I had prayed many, many times for Josie Rose to have a sibling. "But I didn't want it to look like *this*," I contested.

"You wanted a sibling for Josie." God spoke clearly but lovingly again.

He was right. It was an answered prayer. I hung my head nodding in defeated agreement.

I let a few more warm drops fall, but not of sadness more of acceptance. I had learned to trust that God knew best, even when it hurt. I knew I was beginning another journey of trusting Him. Josie would have a brother or sister. It was an answered prayer. It wasn't about me. It was about God blessing Christian, Rachel, and Josie. Something I had prayed for over and over.

After those three days, I chose to be genuinely joyful for Christian and Rachel. I began to pray daily for a healthy pregnancy, an easy delivery, a healthy sibling for Josie, and that this baby would bring so much joy, so much togetherness, and so much love to Christian, Josie, and Rachel. I prayed for strength. I prayed for my heart to love this child. I prayed this child would be a leader in the kingdom and that his or her heart would beat for the Lord. I prayed Nehemiah 8:10 out loud every day, and every day, God met me with the strength needed for that day.

"The joy of the Lord is my strength" (Nehemiah 8:10). Not the joy of my perfect family that is still together. Not the joy of my perfect past. Not the joy of my perfect daughter and perfect bonus kiddos. Not the joy of having more babies. But the joy of the Lord is my strength.

> *"Truly I tell you, whatever you bind on earth will be bound in heaven, and whatever you loose on earth will be loosed in heaven. I now use my words to loose the blessings of God to flow into my life. I fully expect to be overtaken by goodness."*
> **—Matthew 18:18**

Chapter 40

The Final Lie

*"Be alert and of sober mind. Your enemy, the devil,
prowls around like a roaring lion looking for
someone to devour."*

—1 Peter 5:8

It had been one of those days—and not in a good way.
I wanted to just stop. Stop my ministry that God had
blessed me with. Stop trying so hard with my new
bonus kiddos. Stop planning meals and cleaning our new
home that was much larger than I was used to, and most
days seemed to completely overwhelm me. Stop leaving
sweet notes around the house for Tate, and stop trying to
be this phenomenal wife for him. Stop trying to be the fun
upbeat mom to my teenage girlie. I was just worn down.

It had been a challenging two years of transition into
a blended family. I didn't realize how living as a single
mom for eight years would create such selfish routines and
stubborn, set ways. I forgot how emotionally draining it
could be living with someone, especially as a recovering
codependent. I had gone from a family of two where I

was in complete control, to a family of six where I felt completely out of control. I was exhausted from trying too hard. I was being pulled in so many different directions, and I felt like I wasn't super great at any of them.

Before my ministry, my j-o-b-s were stressful at times, and boy, did I have a lot of them. I was a Coffee House Manager, Financial Planner Assistant, Health Insurance Rep, BellSouth Mid-Market Business Development Account Manager, Retail Assistant Manager, Leukemia Lymphoma CMM/Triathlon Division Marketing Coordinator, Real Estate Listing Coordinator, stay-at-home Mom, IT Marketing Manager, and then an IT Business Development Manager. But no matter the position, I always knew my duties and knew if I worked hard, it would pay off. Paid jobs were trackable and measurable. If I did well, I was rewarded monetarily, and I loved closing deals, producing, and working hard.

Ministry was completely different. For the first time in my professional career, I didn't know if I was doing a good job or not. I didn't know if the seeds I was planting were making a difference. Nothing was trackable or measurable. There were no tangible rewards for a good speech given, mentoring a woman in crisis, or an on-point motivational weekly vlog. There was no boss to go to for a pat on the back or a performance review. It was like throwing your wisdom into the wind and hoping something was taking root in someone's heart. And it drove me crazy.

I had been raised with such a deep-rooted work ethic. I came from a long line of hard workers on both my mother and father's side of the family. How could I know that I was being a good steward of the message God had entrusted me with? *Maybe I should just go get a job at something I know I am good at,* I thought to myself. The devil was working on my mind, and at this moment, I felt defeated.

As I stood at the edge of our bed, ready to climb under the sheets, I could hear my husband getting ready in our master bath. Tate and I truly were so blessed. Overall, God had given us an amazing first two years of marriage. Our relationship with one another was so solid. He had redeemed every area of our lives and prospered us in ways we could never have dreamed

---

The devil had messed with the wrong little woman.

I looked behind me to see the moon shining over the lake, gleaming through the trees and through the bedroom window, right at me. A peace came over me, and I felt a God-nudge to check my voicemail.

I was notorious for not checking voicemails as often as I should. Some weeks, I would go days without listening to them, especially if I didn't recognize the number. I picked up my phone and finally decided to listen to a message that I had received the previous Saturday—a good three days prior. *Ooops,* I thought to myself, and I pushed play.

"Hi, sweet Scarlett! This is Amie from Joy Church. Pastor and the board here have decided we would be so honored for you to share your Joy Story with the congregation. Your message is so powerful and so needed. Please give me a call at your convenience to discuss. Blessings!"

In an instant, my eyes filled with tears. I was speechless, overwhelmed with utter disbelief and complete joy at the same moment. *Me? They wanted me? A woman who had committed adultery in a church? They wanted me to share my testimony in front of the congregation?* I collapsed onto the bed in tears and Tate came rushing out of the bathroom to check on me.

"Baby, Are you okay? Who was that?" Tate asked completely puzzled.

I couldn't talk for a few moments. I just shook my head and let the tears gently roll while he held me. I finally was able to mutter, "They want me. They want me, baby. They want me to do a Joy story and share my testimony with the church. I can't believe it. This is it! This is my full-circle healing moment. I just . . . I just never thought it would happen. A church backing my message. A church allowing me to have a voice again. I don't know what to say." Tate smiled as tears filled his eyes, too.

"That is amazing! God is so good, and I am so proud of you."

He was always the first to give glory right back to God after any blessing that came our way. I jumped off the bed to meet him for a hug, and we stood there holding each other and crying, soaking up the goodness of the moment.

We knew we didn't deserve any of it. We knew it was all God, and His incredible grace playing out in our lives.

The final lie had been annihilated. My last fear was destroyed. Satan had continued to hound me and feed my head with his deceptions. With every victory, he would continually tell me that I may be helping a few women here and there, but no church would ever back my message and my ministry. If they knew the *whole story*—that my affair happened in a church—my own church would cast me out.

These were the only deceptions I still had a tough time fending off. But with this news, his final lies and my final fears had been destroyed. Full-circle healing was mine. It was the confirmation I needed and at just the right time. I felt a newfound strength and confidence in my spirit knowing my church was behind me.

The devil had messed with the wrong little woman. It was time for sweet revenge, and there was no stopping me now.

Chapter 41

It's Okay. It's Okay.

"Life doesn't have to be perfect to be wonderful."
—Anonymous.

Josie Rose is fourteen and a half years young.

Ding dong. Our doorbell rang, and Josie ran to see who was at the door. I grinned to myself as I hovered around the kitchen, knowing who she was about to greet.

"It's Dad and Charlie!" She exclaimed with pure excitement in her voice.

She flung open the door, not able to get it open fast enough.

"Hey, buddy!" She declared as she reached to hug her little brother. "What are y'all doing way out here, Dad?"

She had no idea Christian was coming to visit before Christmas. He had called and asked if he could run her ugly sweater by for our upcoming holiday ugly sweater party. I didn't mind, seeing as how it was going to save us from having to purchase another one. "That's a little out of

193

your way, isn't it?" I had challenged him earlier. He said it wasn't a problem because Rachel was working at the clinic, and he had the whole Saturday with Little Man.

"We wanted to come see you before Christmas. That okay with you?" Her dad jested back.

"Of course, it's okay!" She said through a huge smile as she gave her daddy a bear hug.

Charlie was now a year and a couple of months young. He was healthy, precious, and a pure joy to be around. Josie and Charlie took off to the living room to play. Charlie was walking now and on the move. He looked so much like Josie did as a baby that I caught myself staring at him sometimes, lost in his sweet chubby cheeks and big blue eyes.

Christian closed the door. I thanked him again for driving the sweater all the way out. It was a good forty-five-minute trek for him.

"No problem at all. I really wanted to surprise Josie," he stated through his satisfied grin.

After catching up with Josie, Christian started visiting with Tate in the kitchen, while I followed the siblings to the living room. Charlie was toddling around our leather ottoman giggling, while Josie chased him. It was such a treat to see them together interacting and loving on each other. It made my heart so full. God had filled my soul with such adoration and appreciation for little Charlie. I could see how proud Josie was of him and how much responsibility she felt in being a good big sister. It was like witnessing a new layer of love, kindness, and self-esteem unfold in her life. I was so incredibly proud of her.

Christian visited with Tate for almost an hour at the kitchen island while Josie and I enjoyed Charlie. For the first time, I picked up Charlie and took him around to see the shiny ornaments on our tree. While we stood by the mantle looking at stockings, I realized I was living out a vision I'd had nearly nine years ago.

In the vision, I saw myself holding a baby boy in front of a stone mantle, just like our mantle. My heart was so happy and content as I held the child. I had always interpreted that to mean one day *I would have a son*. How else could I feel so happy and so full as I did in the vision? Yet, here I was in this moment, completely satisfied as I held sweet Charlie. As I kissed his forehead, such a calming peace came over me. He was such a sweet boy. And this was such a sweet moment.

I felt elated to be married to Tate and have a thriving ministry where I could help others choose differently than I had, for a better life. I was delighted that Christian was happily married and was able to have another child. I was grateful Rachel was a good wife and a kind bonus mom to Josie. I was overjoyed that Josie had a brother. I no longer had to worry about her being all by herself if ever Christian or I passed away early.

So many surprising triumphs and so much peace surrounded me at that moment. The vision had come to pass and it was more than I could have asked for. I honestly couldn't have dreamed it better if I tried.

Everyone was okay. Tate and I were okay. Josie and her Daddy were okay.

As I bounced Charlie on my hip, I was reminded of those words God spoke calmly to me over a decade ago in Josie's bedroom—it would all be okay. At the time, I didn't understand. I could not see how any of this mess could be okay. But in God's masterful way, He had taken my mess and made it a beautiful message of hope, healing, and redemption. All was okay.

God had blessed us all with double for our trouble. He was indeed steadfast once again, even amongst our brokenness. I could now grasp and agree with what God was telling me then: "It's okay. It's okay."

"I have perfect knowledge and understanding
of every circumstance in life for the spirit of truth
dwells in me."
—Colossians 1:9

Chapter 42

Flourish

*"There is abundant life after huge failure . . .
even if you caused the failure."*
—Scarlett Rose

I had heard it for years: "God will give you double for your trouble!" If I had a dollar for every time I had heard my pastor declare this, I would have a great start to my retirement fund. It sounds nice, doesn't it? But deep down though, I didn't believe it. I remember thinking, *Maybe for those who didn't choose their mess, but I made my mess. I chose all of this. There is no way God can redeem my situation and take my life now giving me double what I used to have!* Yet, here I sit. Typing out the final chapter to my book that has been picked up by a New York Publisher to be re-released as a second edition.

Three years ago, I walked down the sandy beaches of Naples, Florida, in a flowing vintage gown to stand in front of my future husband, and take our vows for our second rodeo. Three months later, we moved into our custom-built dream home in Tennessee, with rolling hills that border the water.

This past summer we put a pool in our back yard oasis. (Something I had only dreamed about having as a child, but never really thought possible.)

My daughter has turned into the most wonderful teenager a mom could ever ask for. I have three lovely, smart, healthy bonus children who are hard workers and great kids. My husband is my best friend, my companion. He is the perfect mate for me. God, in His infinite wisdom, somehow pieced together the biggest messiest mess I could have never dreamed that I would make, and has crafted a masterpiece that I honestly cannot believe is my life.

Because of His great, redeeming love for me, I want to love and serve Him all my days. The only reason I wrote this book, is because He asked me to. He knew you would need this, and that I would need it as well. He knew I needed to have a voice around my mess and He blessed me with a ministry, Choose Different Ministries.

It's my outreach to help those affected by adultery choose better than I did. I teach others that they can learn from me and choose a different path. It's never too late to make a new beginning. There *is* abundant life after failure . . . even if *you* caused the failure.

I have been a featured guest on six Christian television programs that have a combined broadcast reach into 600 million homes through thirty-five broadcast networks across 204 countries—and on seven apps! My testimony has been interpreted into three other languages including

Spanish, Romanian, and Dutch. I have a podcast called "Everyone Has A Voice" that is available on iTunes, Google Play, and Spotify. Here, I am able to help others who have walked through difficult—and often silent—storms have a voice of their own, where they can use their wisdom and experiences to help others. God continues to blow my mind, as He has vindicated every area of my life. He truly took my hot mess and turned it into a hot bless!

I once knew the pain and torment of bondage, but it has been lifted. And freedom has never felt so sweet! In fact, I've never felt this free in my entire life! I am truly okay. God is in the redeeming business. And boy, did He do an excellent work in my life.

As I wrap up the final edits for this book, I'm completely relaxed as I look out of the large, three-paned living-room window to my right. In the backyard, the tall trees sway in the breeze, a beautiful reminder that God is always with me, in each and every detail. I take a deep, cleansing breath and exhale. "It's okay, God," I say with confidence.

It's okay that I had to walk through trauma to gain the amazing life I have.

It's okay I only had one child. Josie brings me the joy of four!

It's okay that my first husband remarried and is thriving with his new wife.

It's okay that Christian and Rachel have a beautiful baby boy together.

It's okay that I am remarried with three bonus children.

It's okay that I had to lose big to be able to help others win big.

I agree and stand with God—it really is okay.

And it will be okay for you, too, because with God, there *is* abundant life after failure.

> *"My cup overflows."*
>
> **— Psalms 23:5**

See What's Next

Watch Christy's JOY Story & Other
TV Interviews at:
ChooseDifferent.org

Download & Listen to Christy's Podcast,
"Everyone Has A Voice" at:
ChooseDifferent.org
Also available on Apple, Google, Spotify, Amazon, and the iHeart App!

Book Christy for a Speaking Engagement,
Church Event, or Youth Event at:
ChooseDifferent.org
And click on "Contact Christy"

Overcome Negative Self-Talk & Declare Victory Over
Your Life with Christy's Mentor Program:
ChooseDifferent.org
And click on "Contact Christy"

Subscribe to Choose Different TV on YouTube at:
ChooseDifferent.org
And click on "Choose Different TV"

You Are Not Alone.

Get Connected!

Facebook.com/choosedifferentministries
Instagram.com/choosedifferent
And on YouTube at Choose Different TV

The Dirty Dozen

12 Warning Signs That You May Be Susceptible to Bad Habits That Can Lead to an Affair:

1. You have a "Daddy-sized hole." Growing up you did not receive adequate attention and affection from your father or father figure.
2. You have a "Mommy-sized hole." Growing up you did not receive adequate attention and affection from your mother or mother figure.
3. You require a lot of attention and reassurance.
4. You dress for someone other than yourself or your spouse (i.e., you find yourself picking out clothes according to what you think someone else would like, or according to what would grab someone else's attention outside of your marriage).
5. You get excited when someone other than your spouse compliments you.
6. You have feelings of unresolved resentment and built-up anger toward your spouse.
7. You have stopped fighting in your marriage and have become indifferent toward your spouse.

8. You tend to be passive-aggressive.

9. You never take time for yourself.

10. You feel poured-out. Your well is dry. The love bank is empty.

11. You often daydream of what it might be like to be with someone else.

12. You hear thoughts like: *You deserve a little fun. Something just for you. Just a season of fun.*

Go to **ChooseDifferent.org** to follow **Choose Different Ministries** Facebook page, **Choose Different** on Instagram and **Choose Different TV** on YouTube for daily motivators, wisdom nuggets, and Christy's Transparent Tuesday videos!

About the Author

Christy Neal is an advocate for women who feel tainted and cast out after adultery. As the author of *Don't Ever Tell* and the podcast host of *Everyone Has A Voice*, Christy is now the catalyst for healing she desperately needed but never found after her own affair over a decade ago. Christy currently resides in Middle Tennessee with her husband and blended family of four amazing kids. She enjoys time with family and friends, staying active, and spoiling her tiny Chihuahua, Riley Woodstock, rotten.